THE DANUBE

GW00384719

JPM GUIDES

From the Black Forest to the Black Sea

Who can hear the name Danube without thinking of that most famous of Strauss waltzes: "On the Beautiful Blue Danube"? Beautiful it certainly is, but to be honest, it's more a brownish yellow than blue, thanks to the lime stirred up from the river bed. The Danube's romance lies in the medieval castles, baroque churches and rococo palaces it passes on its way through central Europe and the Balkans.

The great waterway begins in southwest Germany at the confluence of the Brege and the Brigach, and flows through eight other countries to the sea: Austria, Slovakia, Hungary, Croatia, Serbia, Romania, Bulgaria and Ukraine. Its 2,850 km (1,770

miles) make it Europe's second longest river, after the Volga. Barge traffic starts at the cathedral town of Ulm, larger vessels at Regensburg. Today, completion of the Main–Danube Canal extends navigation from the North Sea to the Black Sea delta, more than 3,200 km (2,000 miles).

The Danube crosses from Germany into Austria at Passau, established as a frontier town by the Romans. It flows through the major port town of Linz to the Habsburgs' grand imperial city of Vienna. From Slovakia's capital, Bratislava, the river follows the Hungarian border until it makes a 90° turn at the dramatic Danube Bend, crossing Hungary's Great Alföld Plain to Budapest. The river cleaves through the city, separating the old hill town of Buda from the more modern Pest.

Beyond the suburbs, the river returns to its bucolic mood, flowing through flat, fertile countryside. In all, the Danube stretches 417 km (260 miles) through Hungary.

The section between Budapest and the Black Sea has always been inextricably entangled with the history of the region. Roman sentries and Dacian warriors kept watch on each other across the lower Danube, as did centuries later the armies of the Habsburgs and the Ottoman Turks. Many of the towns were founded in Roman times, and medieval fortresses, castle ruins and memorials still attest to the battles which were fought here. Under the Austro-Hungarian Monarchy (1683–1918), the countries on the middle and lower reaches seemed to be united—the first and only time that a "Confederation of the Danube" has been a reality.

On its way to the Black Sea, the river passes through an incredibly varied landscape. In the Great Hungarian Plain (Nagy Alföld) it is joined by major tributaries: the Drava, the Sava and the Tisza. Flooding has produced a remarkable zone of woods, ponds and streams, now protected as the nature reserves.

The Danube achieves its greatest breadth below Belgrade. Further south, spectacular landscapes await the voyager, as the river cuts a gorge through the Southern Carpathian Mountains at the narrow gorge of the Iron Gate. A hydroelectric power plant was built here in 1971, making a major impact on the natural environment, but a positive result was that this stretch of the river, previously feared for its cataracts, became navigable for ships. From the Iron Gate the river flows into the lowlands of Walachia, where it is hemmed on the Bulgarian side by craggy mountain spurs, whilst the opposite, Romanian bank is flat and marshy. The Danube turns northward before the Dobrogea tableland, to turn back eastward at Galaţi. After this final dogleg the delta begins.

The Danubian region is a veritable mosaic of peoples. The ancestors of today's Romanians were Dacians and Romans; those of the Bulgarians were Slavs and Thracians. The Germans too have had an impact on the culture of the region: in the 12th century, King Géza of Hungary brought Saxons into Transylvania, and in the 18th century Empress Maria Theresa of Austria settled Swabians on the lower Danube to revitalize and cultivate deserted lands. The political upheavals of the 20th century forced the majority of these settlers to return to their former homeland.

3

Early times	*Homo Palaeohungaricus,* a very primitive version of a human, settles in Hungary, attracted by the hot springs and abundance of water and wildlife. Trade along the Danube develops as early as the Neolithic. The original inhabitants of Bulgaria, the Thracians, spread to the lands between the lower Danube and the northern Aegean around 1000 BC.
5th–2nd centuries BC	Celts settle in on the River Sava and on the middle Danube and in the 3rd century BC built a fortress on the site of the future Belgrade. Under pressure from the Romans, the Germanic peoples and the Iranian Sarmatians, Celtic domination is broken around 120 BC. In present-day Romania, the Dacian kingdom is born.
1st century BC	From 27 BC, under Emperor Augustus, Roman conquest of the Danube Valley makes the river (*Danubius,* and in its lower reaches, the *Ister*) the empire's northern border against barbarians—Celts, Pannonians and Illyrians. Some 20,000 Roman soldiers are deployed along the river between Vienna and Budapest. Roman towns are founded, including Castra Regina (Regensburg), Vindobona (Vienna), Aquincum (Budapest) and Singidunum (Belgrade).
1st–3rd centuries AD	In the 1st century AD, the Danube forms the northern frontier of the Roman Empire; the line of fortifications (the Limes) running along the river is intended to protect the Empire from barbarian incursions. Further important riverside fortresses such as Ratiaria (Vidin) and Nicopolis ad Istrum (Nikopol) are built at the mouths of tributaries. In AD 106, Emperor Trajan defeats the Dacians and so conquers the lower reaches of the Danube. In the 3rd century, Goths penetrate southwards as far as the Danube but are defeated by Tacitus. In the 4th century, the frontier must once again be defended against Goths and Sarmatians.
4th–9th centuries AD	Major invasions take place but also peaceful settlement. In the 4th and 5th centuries, Germanic tribes overrun the Danubian region and weaken the Roman Empire. The Huns appear in Pannonia in the 5th century. In the 6th and 7th centuries, the Slavs expand their territories,

and in the lands which today form Bulgaria they intermingle with the Thracian population. In the 8th century Emperor Charlemagne drives out the Goths, and Attila's Huns and Avars who came from the Asian steppes. However, Magyars from somewhere between the Volga river and the Ural mountains settle in Hungary along with a few Turkic Petchenegs and Curmans.

10th–14th centuries	Ten tribes—seven Hungarian and three Khazar—unite to defend themselves from menacing Petchenegs, Russians and Bulgars. Prince Arpád, head of the Magyars, is named supreme leader. Hungary's conversion to Christianity in 975, initiated under a great-grandson of Arpád, Prince Géza, makes the Danube a safe overland route for pilgrims going to the Holy Land. Géza's son Stephen is crowned in 1000 the first king of Hungary. Canonized after his death, Stephen becomes the country's patron saint. The river proves rather more perilous when French and German Crusaders choose it in 1096 for their pillaging progress through Austria and Hungary to "save" Constantinople and Jerusalem from Islam. England's Richard I the Lion-Heart is imprisoned in Dürnstein Castle on his way home from Palestine in 1192. In 1396, an army of 100,000 Germans, French, Hungarians, Poles, Bohemians, Italians and Spaniards congregates at Budapest and advances down the Danube—to meet crushing defeat by the Turks at Nicopolis, now Nikopol in Bulgaria.
15th century	The Viceroy of Hungary, János Hunyadi, repels Turkish invaders (1456) at Nándorfehérvár (now Belgrade). His son, the "just king" Matthias I Corvinus, reigns from 1458 to 1490, an intellectual golden age.
16th–18th centuries	In the 16th century, the Danube becomes the route of a "crusade" in reverse, as Suleiman the Magnificent's Ottoman Turks carry Islam west from the Black Sea. After the battle of Mohács in 1526, Hungary falls to the Ottomans for 150 years, but they do not succeed in pushing westwards to Vienna. Serbia, Bosnia and parts of Romania also fall under Ottoman rule. The Habsburgs gradually reconquer these lands: Hungary in 1687 and

5

Transylvania in 1691. The Treaty of Karlowitz (Sremski Karlovci) ends the war against the Turks in 1699 and makes Austria the major power in the Danube region.

Under Maria Theresa (1740-80) the peoples of the Danube are united. The Empress moves German settlers into the areas left deserted after the expulsion of the Turks. But the Turks are not completely beaten yet: in the Russo-Turkish War of 1768–74 Russia occupies the principalities of Moldavia and Walachia, and in the Treaty of Svištov (1791), Austria gains the Iron Gate pass on the Danube near Orsova.

19th century	Russia conducts further wars against Turkey, some of them in the Danubian region. In the Treaty of Adrianople (Edirne) in 1829, almost all of the Danube delta is ceded to Russia. In 1829 the Danube Steamship Company is founded. In the Treaty of Paris (1856) Russia loses control of shipping on the Danube, which is declared open to international traffic. Thanks to the historic battle between the Russians and the Turks at Pleven, Bulgaria becomes an independent state.
20th century– present	After World War I the Austro-Hungarian Monarchy collapses (1918); the Danube lands become independent states. In 1932 a conference on Danubian affairs is held in London. The French prime minister Tardieu suggests unification of the Danubian region (excepting Germany and Italy), but his plan falls through. In World War II, the Danube becomes a front line. German naval forces use the river to reach the Black Sea. The victorious Soviet army occupies Budapest, Belgrade, Transylvania, Walachia and the Banat in 1944, and introduces a Communist regime. The USSR thus achieves supremacy in the Danubian region and the Balkans. The fall of the Berlin Wall in 1989 has far-reaching consequences for all the states on the middle and lower Danube. Hungary and Slovakia join the EU in 2004.

The Old Town Hall of Bamberg, on an island in the Regnitz River, was begun in the 15th century.

Main–Danube Canal

In 1992 the boldest dreams of Charlemagne and Ludwig I of Bavaria were realised when the Main–Danube Canal between Bamberg and Kelheim was completed, opening to seagoing ships a 3,500-km (2,170-mile) waterway linking the North Sea with the Black Sea.

Work on the canal began in the Middle Ages—a considerable technical achievement, though it remained unfinished.

The Ludwigskanal, with 100 locks punctuating its 177-km (110-mile) length, was inaugurated with pomp in 1846, but increasing competition from the railways proved disastrous. Further work was undertaken in 1922, the stretch from Bamberg to Nuremberg became navigable in 1972, and in 1992 the final stretch to Kelheim was inaugurated. The resulting canal is 171 km (106 miles) long, has 16 locks, and at Hilpoltstein reaches 406 m (1,332 ft) above

sea level, the highest point on the European waterway network.

Cruises from the Main to the Danube begin in **Würzburg**, a proud episcopal city straddling the River Main amid the charming vine-clad slopes of Franconia. One of the highlights of any tour of the city is the 18th-century Residenz of the prince-bishops: Balthasar Neumann created here one of the most beautiful baroque palaces in Europe. The frescoes over the ceremonial staircase and in the Kaisersaal (Imperial Hall) were created by the Venetian Tiepolo. The Dom (cathedral) dates back to the 11th–13th centuries and was extensively rebuilt after World War II. It has three works by the famous Würzburg sculptor Tilman Riemenschneider. North of the cathedral stands the Neumünsterkirche with a baroque façade attributed to Johann Dientzenhofer. On the other bank of the Main, across the picturesque Alte Mainbrücke (Old Main Bridge, 1473–1543), the Marienberg fortress looms over the town. Dating in part from the 13th century, it contains the Main-fränkisches Museum and works by Riemenschneider.

About 20 km (12½ miles) upstream from Würzburg you reach **Ochsenfurt**, whose town walls date back to the 14th century. The Andreaskirche (13th–15th centuries) has a richly decorated interior with a sculpture by Tilman Riemenschneider.

The former importance of **Kitzingen**, one of the oldest towns on the Main (8th century), is apparent from its Renaissance town hall and several churches dating from the 15th to 18th centuries. Parts of the town walls still remain.

The attractive little wine-growing town of **Volkach**, on a loop of the Main, is worth a visit for its fine Renaissance town hall and the baroque Schelfenhaus, but especially for the pilgrim church of St Maria im Weingarten (St Mary-in-the-Vineyard) to the northwest of the town, which boasts Riemenschneider's Rosenkranzmadonna (Madonna of the Rosary).

Schweinfurt is the biggest industrial centre of Lower Franconia. The city has been destroyed several times over the centuries, most recently in World War II. Nevertheless, some buildings remain to attest to its historic importance as a free imperial city, among them the late-Romanesque Johanniskirche (altered several times), the town hall (16th century), the former Gymnasium (grammar school), now the town museum, and the Zeughaus (armoury).

The delightful Franconian town of **Hassfurt** lies 28 km (17 miles) further on. Its late-Gothic Ritterkapelle (Knights' Chapel) boasts a heraldic frieze with 241 coats of arms, together with interesting tombs. The Gothic Pfarrkirche (parish church) contains several works of art, including a wooden sculpture of John the Baptist by Tilman Riemenschneider.

Only 30 km (18½ miles) to go until you reach the episcopal city of **Bamberg**. This is where the Main–Danube Canal begins. The old town is graced with works by the sculptor Riemenschneider and the architect family Dientzenhofer. Take a good look at the cathedral, Bamberg's greatest attraction, where the transition from Romanesque to Gothic can be clearly traced. It houses the tomb of Emperor Heinrich II and his wife, a work of Riemenschneider's, as well as the *Bamberger Reiter*, a remarkable Gothic equestrian statue. On Karolinenplatz stand the late-Gothic Alte Hofhaltung (the former episcopal palace, now housing the historical museum) and the early baroque Neue Hofhaltung (also called the Neue Residenz). The latter, designed by J.L. Dientzenhofer, has on the first floor a gallery of paintings by German masters, and on the second you can admire grand chambers with antique furniture and tapestries. There's a fine view of the old town and the Benedictine abbey of St Michael from the rose garden. On an island in the River Regnitz, which once separated the castle district from the bourgeois quarter, stands the Altes 9

Rathaus (Old Town Hall), decorated with 18th-century frescoes. The picturesque fishing quarter of "Little Venice" *(Klein Venedig)* lies on the right-hand bank of the river.

Make a side-trip to **Bayreuth**, known for its annual festival of Richard Wagner's operas. The composer's home, Villa Wahnfried, is now a museum containing stage sets, costumes and musical memorabilia. Wagner is buried in the garden with his wife Cosima, daughter of Liszt. The Markgräfliches Opernhaus, by two theatre designers from Bologna in the 18th century, is a charming baroque creation, with three galleries festooned in stucco trimmings.

Nuremberg, virtually destroyed in World War II, has been lovingly restored, and its churches, museums and culinary delicacies are incentives to spend some time here.

The small Bavarian town of **Berching** greets the visitor with a skyline straight out of the Middle Ages: the town ramparts (constructed around 1450), with 13 towers and four gates, are intact, and you can walk along some sections of the walls.

The present-day health resort **Riedenburg** on the River Altmühl became a market town in the 13th century, protected by three castles. The valley of the Altmühl is popular with nature lovers, hikers, canoeists and cyclists alike. The Jagdfalkenhof (Falconry Lodge) at Schloss Rosenburg (built 1112) gives daily demonstrations with large birds of prey.

At **Kelheim** the Altmühl flows into the Danube, and here ends the Main–Danube Canal. The remains of the medieval walls and gates of this town, founded around 1200, can still be seen. Note the Gothic parish church and the elegant façades of the baroque town houses. To the west of Kelheim, the 45-m (147-ft) Befreiungshalle (Liberation Hall), built by Ludwig I of Bavaria to commemorate the wars of liberation fought against Napoleon, crowns the Michelsberg.

The Benedictine monastery of **Weltenburg** stands in a setting full of natural drama, where the Danube breaks a narrow gorge through the hills of the Franconian Alb. This is where the Christianization of Bavaria is supposed to have begun in the 7th century. The monastery church, a late-baroque jewel, was built in 1716–18 by the Asam brothers, who were active in south Germany but also further afield in Bohemia and Silesia. Earthly pleasures are catered for by the beer from the monastery-run brewery.

Like Bamberg, **Regensburg** survived the war unscathed, revealing itself in full historical splendour. The city hails back to Roman times, when the mighty Porta Praetoria was built: it stands near the cathedral. The diocese was founded in the 8th century, and from this time princes and emperors held their Diets in the city. Regensburg's heyday was the Middle Ages, and to this day the magnificence of the merchants' houses attests to their wealth and prestige. The Steinerne Brücke (Stone Bridge) is the oldest surviving bridge in Germany (12th-century), and connects the main part of the city with the settlement on the other bank of the Danube. The beautiful old city is dominated by the magnificent Petersdom cathedral, with its two 105-m (344-ft) towers, the *pièce de résistance* of Gothic architecture in Bavaria. The cathedral houses many treasures. The church of St Emmeram dates back to the 8th century but has the Asam brothers to thank for its sumptuous baroque interior. The finest secular building in the city is probably the Old Town Hall.

Regensburg is also a city of good Bavarian cooking: the Alte Wurstküche (Old Sausage Kitchen) is believed to be Germany's oldest restaurant!

A short distance downstream, a huge pseudo-Grecian temple towers above the Danube, resplendent in white marble: this is **Walhalla**, built for Ludwig I of Bavaria. Climb the 358 marble steps from the moorings to the temple, which houses busts of eminent Germans.

Straubing lies in the fertile Dungau, the heart of the Bavarian granary. Every August, the town is the scene of a lively two-week festival. In the picturesque Altstadt (Old Town), see the 14th-century Stadtturm with its five spires on Hauptplatz; Theresienplatz and Ludwigsplatz are surrounded by elegant patrician houses. One of the finest churches is the Ursulinenkirche, designed by the Asam brothers. Straubing's oldest place of worship is a short distance out of town: the Peterskirche, built around 1200. One of the churchyard's three chapels is devoted to Agnes Bernauer, a barber's daughter who fell in love with Duke Albrecht III of Bavaria, and was drowned as a witch in the Danube when Albrecht's father got wind of their unsuitable marriage.

Austria is but a stone's throw away from the "Town of Three Rivers", **Passau**, at the confluence of the Danube, Inn and Ilz. Ships moor below the proud Veste Oberhaus castle. 11

KEY

Motorway
Highway
Secondary road
Railway
Frontier
✈ International airport
▪ Castle, Fortress
◻ Ruins
◻ Church

Distances on the Danube are measured in kilometres starting at Sulina on the delta, km 0.

Passau to Budapest

At its crossing point from Germany into Austria, the Danube is joined by two other rivers, the sturdy Inn from the south and the little Ilz from the north. Champions of the Inn (which gives its name to Innsbruck) note that it is broader and bluer here than the Danube, and so much more deserving of Johann Strauss's waltz.

Passau (km 2227), the town that straddles the confluence of the three rivers, is a solid old bishopric that has always enjoyed the good life, celebrating its religious festivities with plenty of music, beer for the men and hot chocolate for the ladies. Historically prospering from the trades in wine, wheat and salt, it is an inviting city, from the bulbous onion domes and graceful arches of its baroque monuments to the rounded promontories separating the waterways. For a fine view over the town's charming backdrop of green wooded hillsides, make your way up to the Oberhaus fortress. The castle museum offers a good introduction to the region's art and craftwork—of old, Passau rivalled Damascus and Toledo for the delicate workmanship of its finely honed sword blades. Exhibits also trace the history of shipping on the Danube.

Over to the south, the core of the town stands on the ridge of land between the Danube and

Inn rivers. Towering over it is the cathedral of St Stephan, with its three onion domes, Flamboyant Gothic chancel, rich baroque interior boasting a total of 1,000 sculpted figures, and the world's biggest church organ, with 17,774 pipes.

Standing where the valley flattens into a plain, on a major crossroads to Germany and the Czech Republic, **Linz** (km 2135) is capital of the province of Upper Austria and centre of the country's heavy industry. Back in 1832, it was the starting point of Austria's first "railway"—with horses providing the locomotive power, pulling wagons to Budweis in Bohemia. Five years later, the first steamship moored here. Today, the huge VOEST steel plant is located across the Nibelung Bridge on the north bank, along with important chemical factories. The port, separated from the river by a protective harbour with special wharves, is Austria's biggest, handling 5 million tonnes of goods per year.

The old city is nicely preserved on the south bank, cen-

PASSAU'S PACIFISTS

The people of Passau have always been far too fond of the good life to spoil it by wasting time fighting. When the town was besieged by the Bavarians in 1703, the bishop's three companies of soldiers declined to report for duty, explaining that they had all come down with a fever. The Bavarian forces were eventually able to complete their conquest, but not until 1741—and their general, much frustrated, complained that he had met no opposition at all!

13

tred around a main square (Hauptplatz) surrounded by handsome houses of the 17th and 18th centuries and an imposing Gothic Rathaus (town hall). In the centre of the square is the tall, twisting Dreifaltigkeitssäule (Trinity Pillar), set up in 1723 to commemorate the town's deliverance from ten years of war, fire and plague.

ADOPTIVE SONS

If it prefers to forget that Adolf Hitler spent several years of his youth in Linz (and dreamt of ending his days here), the town is proud to celebrate the great 17th-century astronomer Johannes Kepler, who taught at the university, and 19th-century composer Anton Bruckner, the town's organist. It also has links with Mozart who created his *Linzer Symphonie* here in 1783.

The square's grand baroque Jesuitenkirche is known locally as the "old cathedral", having served as such till 1909. Its façade is graced by statues of three Jesuit heroes, Ignatius Loyola, Francis Xavier and Francis Borgia (a rare saintly figure in that notorious family). It was here that Anton Bruckner (1824–96) played the organ. The oldest church in town, perhaps in all Austria, is Martinskirche on Römerstrasse, dating back at least to Emperor Charlemagne in 799. The 16th-century seat of government on Klosterstrasse, the Landhaus, is a gracious Renaissance building, notable for the flower-bedecked balconies of its arcaded courtyard. The provincial museum, housed in the remains of the old castle, is devoted to local history and exhibitions of modern

art. For a good view of the surrounding countryside and the Alps, an electric railway climbs to the top of the Pöstlingberg over on the north bank.

Mauthausen (km 2112), originally established as an imperial customs station at the confluence with the Enns river, is now more bitterly remembered as the site of Austria's largest concentration camp. A chapel and a monument commemorate its 100,000 victims. The stone quarries where slave labour cut granite for Vienna's building material are now the setting for an international sculpture symposium.

One of the most romantic stretches of the Danube is the **Wachau**, winding its way just 30 km (19 miles) between Melk and Krems. Friendly country villages flanked with apricot orchards and vineyards alternate with dark castle ruins on craggy cliffs. Some of Austria's best white wines and potent *Marillenbrand* (apricot brandy) are nurtured here, along with the passionate, murderous legends of the Nibelungs that inspired Richard Wagner's operas.

The handsome castle of Greinburg watches over the little town of **Grein** (km 2079), which has a lovely rococo theatre in the main square, unaltered since it was built in 1790.

Long before **Melk** (km 2036) became the home of the Benedictines in 1089, its clifftop position above the river bend made it an ideal military camp from which to fend off barbarians. Elegant as it now is, the 18th-century abbey you see today still looks a lot like a fortress, built where the Baben- 15 bergs had previously sited their own palace stronghold. In 1702, architect Jakob Prandtauer was commissioned to transform the forbidding strategic fortification into a splendid baroque sanctuary with gracefully tapering towers and a majestic octagonal dome.

Dürnstein (km 2009) is famous above all for the medieval dungeon where Richard I the Lion-Heart was held prisoner on his return from the Crusades. It cost England 23,000 kg of silver to secure his release. In 1645, during the Thirty Years' War, the Swedes left the hillside castle in ruins. Be sure to visit the town's cheerful baroque abbey church.

Krems (km 2002), the centre of the Wachau's wine industry, has retained an old-town charm. Gothic pepperpot towers greet you at the 15th-century Steiner Tor (city gate). Another Gothic masterpiece is the older Gozzo-Burg patrician residence on Hoher Markt, the town's oldest square. The museum housed in the old Dominikanerkirche displays the medieval art and history of Krems. The 17th-century Veitskirche (Church of St Vitus) is an attractive baroque edifice by Italian architects, with altar paintings by Franz Anton Maulpertsch and frescoes by Martin Johann ("Kremser") Schmidt. But for many, the most enjoyable monuments are the Renaissance houses on Obere Landstrasse, where they serve the new *Heuriger* wine in tree-shaded courtyards.

The Augustine abbey at **Klosterneuburg** (km 1939) was founded in 1114 and rebuilt by Emperor Karl VI in the 18th century to emulate the Escorial in Madrid, home of his Spanish Habsburg ancestors. His dream of a vast palace-cum-church with nine domes, each graced with a Habsburg crown, had to stop short at one big dome, with the imperial crown, and one little one, with the crown of the Austrian archduke. The major

attraction of the interior is the Leopold Chapel's superb 12th-century Verdun Altar with its 45 Biblical scenes painted in enamel panels. As in Krems, the other attraction is outside, in the wine gardens set amid the vineyards at the edge of the Wienerwald (Vienna Woods).

The population of **Vienna** (km 1929), Austria's capital, reflects the cosmopolitan mix of peoples once ruled by the Habsburg Empire: Hungarians, Germans, Czechs, Slovaks, Poles, Spaniards, Flemings and Italians—as a glance in the phone book will confirm. They have all made a contribution to the city's architecture, music and painting, but also to the cuisine of its restaurants and cafés.

Even if you don't have tickets for a performance, take a look at the Staatsoper (opera house) which the Viennese could scarcely wait to rebuilt after the destruction of World War II, the Burgtheater (national theatre) or the magnificent concert halls of the Musikverein and Konzerthaus. So sacred are the performing arts in Vienna, that the atmosphere in the opera house and concert halls is as hallowed as in a Christian cathedral or a Buddhist temple. Not that the towering St Stephen's Cathedral is denied pride of place in the centre of town. Defying eight centuries of war and fire, it remains a grandiose Gothic monument that expresses the city's spirit with both exuberance and dignity. Inside, be sure to see Anton Pilgram's beautifully sculpted Gothic pulpit.

Around the cathedral are monuments large and small. Wolfgang Amadeus Mozart 17 lived in the modest Mozarthaus Vienna (closed until January 2006), Domgasse 5. Vienna's oldest tavern, the Griechenbeisl at Fleischmarkt 11, was a popular haunt of Beethoven and Schubert. The imperial glories of the Habsburgs are housed in their vast Hofburg palace, with its Renaissance and baroque royal apartments, library, chapel and stables for the renowned Spanish Riding School.

Two great museums: the Kunsthistorisches, famous for its Breughels, Dürers and Titians; and the Belvedere Palace devoted mainly to Austrian art of the 19th and 20th centuries. Schönbrunn, the Habsburgs' summer palace, is worth a visit as much for its lovely gardens as for the sumptuous apartments.

To the south of Vienna lies **Gumpoldskirchen**, one of the region's most charming wine-growing villages, and home of the famous white wine of that name. Be sure to visit the 16th-century Rathaus, the Gothic church and local inns offering the new wine, the "Heuriger".

The Cistercian abbey of **Heiligenkreuz** was founded in the 12th century. Its arcaded courtyard had to be rebuilt after an attack by the Turks, but the Romanesque nave and the basilica's Gothic choir remained intact. The Plague Column (*Pestsäule*) in the courtyard and the skilfully carved choir stalls are by the baroque artist Giuliani. The cloister, with its red marble pillars, exudes peace and harmony.

Mayerling achieved its claim to fame through a tragic event: the 30-year-old Crown Prince Rudolf and the 17-year-old Hungarian countess Maria Vetsera committed suicide together in the hunting lodge—their relationship had been condemned as scandalous, and Rudolf had been officially refused a divorce. Emperor Franz Joself had a Carmelite convent built on the spot where the couple died, and Maria Vetsera was buried in the cemetery of Heiligenkreuz, while Rudolf was laid to rest in the family tomb in Vienna.

Capital of Slovakia, **Bratislava** (km 1868) commands a key position close to Austria and Hungary. The new Danube–Oder canal links it to trade with Poland and eastern Germany. Following the Turkish capture of Budapest, Bratislava was the capital-in-exile for Hungary's kings and archbishops from 1541 to 1784. Today, its textile, chemical, oil and metal industries are offset by pleasant forests, vineyards and farmland surrounding a handsome baroque city centre. Towering over the town is the royal castle dating back to the 9th century, rebuilt in the 13th, but now largely Renaissance in style. It houses the Slovak National Museum. Hungarian coronations were held in St Martin's Gothic cathedral. The baroque palaces and town hall date from the golden Habsburg era of Maria Theresa.

Esztergom (km 1718), some 150 km (93 miles) southeast of Bratislava, was Hungary's first capital and royal seat under the Árpád kings. Its Maria-Valeria bridge, which joins the town to Slovakian Sturovo, reopened only in 2001; residents on both banks of the Danube had a long wait for its reconstruction after it was bombed in 1944.

King Stephen was born here around 970, and founded the cathedral in 1010. The monarchy moved out after the Mongol invasions of the 13th century, but the archbishops stayed on, taking over the royal residence. Esztergom was to pay for its ecclesiastical importance in 1543, when it was destroyed by the Turks. The restoration needed was so considerable that the 19

Church only moved back again in 1820. And despite its clergy facing brutal persecution by the Communist authorities in the 1950s and 60s, the city has remained the centre of Hungarian Catholicism.

The gigantic neoclassical basilica that towers over the city skyline is on the site of King Stephen's original cathedral. Begun in 1822, it took nearly 40 years to complete. The dome is based on St Peter's in Rome.

The most outstanding feature of the voluminous interior is the Bakócz Chapel, built in red marble by Florentine Renaissance craftsmen in the early 16th century. It's the only part of the old cathedral left.

To the right of the main altar, the treasury contains a magnificent collection of textiles and medieval gold relics, including the 13th-century Coronation Cross used by Hungary's kings to pledge their oaths up to the last coronation—Charles IV—in 1916. In the crypt is the tomb of Cardinal Mindszenty. He opposed the Communist takeover after the war and was arrested and tortured. Released during the 1956 Uprising, he took refuge in the US Embassy for the next 15 years. He died in exile in 1975 and was reburied with a state funeral in 1991.

You can complete your tour of the church by ascending the cupola for a superb view of both town and river. You'll need lots of energy to tackle the last stage: a narrow, spiral staircase, interminable but worthwhile.

The Castle Museum incorporates parts of the royal palace, including a 12th-century chapel and medieval Hall of Virtues,

named after its frescoes depicting Moderation, Justice, Prudence and Fortitude.

Below the hill are the attractive baroque streets of the **Viziváros**, or Watertown. The Parish Church dates from 1738 and is in Italianate baroque style. In the old Primate's Palace, the Christian Museum houses what ranks as Hungary's greatest collection of religious art, with Italian prints, Renaissance paintings and the ornate 15th-century Garamszentbenedek coffin.

Beautiful green wooded hill country at a hairpin bend in the river just before the famous **Danube Bend** provides an idyllic setting for the remains of King Matthias Corvinus's opulent 15th-century palace at **Visegrad** (km 1695). Much of the sprawling residence—terraced into five levels on the hillside—

has been restored. The monumental Hercules Fountain is a fine example of Hungarian Renaissance; the Court of Honour has graceful arcades.

Vác (km 1679) has a pretty baroque centre, its houses still painted green, red and ochre, compensating for the textile factories and cement works on the outskirts. The 18th-century cathedral boasts some remarkable frescoes by Franz Anton Maulpertsch, while the Triumphal Arch (1764) was purpose-built specially for a visit by Empress Maria Theresa.

Szentendre (km 1668) is a photogenic little town with a surprising quantity of art galleries and museums. Founded by Serbian refugees fleeing the Turks after the Battle of Kosovo in 1389, it received a second wave of Serbs three centuries later when the Turks recaptured Belgrade.

The main town square is the baroque Fő tér, with a votive cross put up by Serbian merchants in 1763 to celebrate the non-appearance of the plague. Here, too, is the green-spired Greek Orthodox Blagoveštenska Church, built ten years earlier. The icons inside are emphatically Serbian, and evoke the troubled history of that land.

Just behind the square's east side, an alley leads to the Margit

Kovács Museum. Kovács, who died in 1977, created stylized, elongated sculptures from ceramics, and her work—part reinvention of religious iconic art, part folksy kitsch—is both striking and entertaining.

Leading south from Fő tér, Dumtsa Jeno utca has two excellent museums. The Barcsay Museum has architectural paintings, mosaics and tapestries by Transylvanian artist Jeno Barcsay. An altogether lighter confection can be enjoyed at the Marzipan Museum, where those with a sweet tooth can lick their lips over such items as a marzipan sculpture of the Parliament.

Until the 19th century, the Hungarian capital **Budapest** (km 1647) was two cities separated by the Danube, hilly Buda on the west bank and flat Pest to the east. Each part has retained its character: Buda with its quiet streets around the splendid Matthias Church and the Royal Palace; Pest, the boisterous centre of the modern city.

Budapest to Mohács

All the towns along the Danube shores have their historic vestiges—perhaps a church built on the remains of a mosque, or the ruins of an ancient monastery. Even the prosaic industrial town **Dunaújváros** (km 1578), the "Danube New Town" constructed around a port and steel mills, has historical treasures to offer, with a park displaying ancient ruins and a museum dedicated to the Roman fortifications unearthed here.

The importance of **Dunaföldvár** (km 1561) is due to its road and rail bridge across the Danube. **Harta** (km 1546) on the left bank dates back to Swabian (German) settlers brought here by Empress Maria Theresa in the 18th century. Further downstream in **Paks** (km 1531) is to be found Hungary's one and only nuclear power station.

The farming town of **Kalocsa** (km 1515) has something for every taste—history, folklore, art, and one of Europe's most offbeat museums. Kalocsa was founded in the 11th century

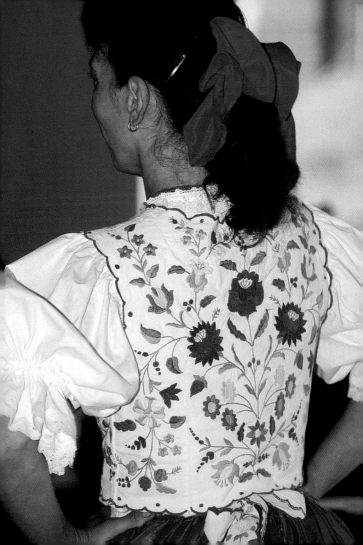

alongside the Danube, but the river subsequently changed its mood and its course, leaving the town 6 km from the nearest fish or boat. Happily, the newly enlarged boundaries of Kalocsa included fertile meadows, where fruit and vegetables and grain grow. The dominant crop, though, is paprika. So it is that Kalocsa offers the Paprika Museum, where you can follow the saga of the Mexican hot pepper through its Hungarian naturalization. It didn't become an essential ingredient of the Hungarian diet until the early 19th century. One of the town's most photogenic features is the display, every autumn, of bright red peppers hanging to dry from the eaves of local houses. On a less romantic note, one of Kalocsa's principal employers is a giant paprika factory.

The Károly Viski Museum is one of the many folklore collections scattered around the country; in the case of Kalocsa there's no shortage of exhibits. The peasant costumes are a delight of floral designs—even the boys sport a splash of colour embroidered on their white shirts. Here, too, are displays of

A garden to wear: embroidered blouses are part of the traditional costume.

traditional farm tools, antique furniture and decorations.

The Kalocsa Folk Art Cooperative has its own museum, also devoted to antique agricultural implements and rustic home furnishings. Kalocsa embroidery is on show—and on sale—and they stage folklore exhibitions in which the local youngsters dance to typically vivacious Hungarian music.

Kalocsa's main square, Szabadság tér, features statues of two national heroes—King (Saint) Stephen and Franz Liszt. The 18th-century cathedral, in graceful baroque style, stands on the site of a series of churches, going back to the 11th century. In the Archbishop's Palace, across the square, the library contains more than 100,000 volumes, including a Bible autographed by Martin Luther.

The centre of a wine-growing region, the county seat of **Szekszárd**, more than 20 km (12 miles) from the river, has a high proportion of citizens of German and Serbian descent. Their pedigree can be traced back to the 150 years of Turkish occupation, when Szekszárd was a ghost town. To renew the population in the 18th century, settlers from neighbouring countries were welcomed. Local history starts in the 11th century, when King Béla I founded a 25 fortified Benedictine monastery on a hill. The courtyard of the present County Hall is built around the remains of an ancient chapel and the abbey church.

If an invader wanted to split Hungary in half he could hardly do better than put out of commission the vulnerable Danube

bridge at **Baja** (km 1479), the southernmost in Hungary. The vital link between east and west Hungary carries rail traffic as well as cars and trucks (eastbound and westbound alternate), all on a single lane. Long before there was a bridge, the Turkish invaders, aware of the strategic significance, fortified the town. Today the enormous main square, Béke tér, gives an idea of the historic importance of Baja.

There are only two ways to visit the 14,000-ha (35,000-acre) game reserve of **Gemenc**, along both banks of the Danube near Baja: by boat or special narrow-gauge train. The area of forested moorland, crisscrossed by backwater loops of the river, is the home of deer, wild boar and a world of bird-life. Keen eyes may sight eagles, falcons, egrets or black storks. The reserve's Hunting Museum contains details of the region's fauna.

The Danube port city of **Mohács** (km 1448) is forever linked with a melancholy chapter in Hungarian history. It unfolded swiftly, a few kilometres out of town, on August 29, 1526. A well-equipped army of Sultan Suleiman the Magnificent, with a four-to-one advantage in manpower, crushed the defending forces of the Hungarian King Louis II. The king died during the retreat. For the next century and a half Hungary endured Ottoman occupation.

The modern Votive Church in the centre of town is one of the local memorials to these events. Meant to give thanks for the eventual expulsion of the Turks, it might be mistaken for a mosque, but the dome is topped by a big cross.

On the actual site of the 16th-century battle, a memorial park is strewn with haunting modern sculptures symbolizing the opposing forces in the disastrous conflict. Here the ghosts of the generals, the soldiers and the horses—in imaginative wood-carvings—are forever deployed across the field of battle. The park was dedicated in 1976 on the 450th anniversary of an unforgettable defeat.

One way the people of Mohács celebrate the departure of the Turks is at Carnival time, when they parade in the scariest giant masks. The Busó carnival, the most spectacular folkloric manifestation in the country, also aims to expel another invader—winter.

The Hungarian version of the wild west—the puszta—conjures visions of gallant horsemen, lonely shepherds, pastures and dunes. It's all still there in **Kiskunság National Park**,

35,000 protected hectares (86,000 acres) of dramatic landscape between the Danube and the Tisza. Accomplished horsemen in baggy trousers and red waistcoats show the tourists their skills in a cross between a rodeo and a circus. Apart from the handsome horses there are herds of big-horned cattle and Racka sheep with screw-shaped horns. The birds that follow include red herons, great egrets and spoonbills.

One of the highlights of a visit to the puszta is a stop at a *czárda*, or wayside inn, where the food is as rustic as the surroundings. The meal is washed down with hearty Hungarian wine and music—including, perhaps, the wail of gypsy violins, or the spirited melodies of the *czárdás*.

HUNGARIAN WINES

Hungary will keep the most demanding wine-lover in a state of bliss. It's a huge producer of quality wines, though few are household names abroad. The renowned Tokaji (also spelt Tokay) as the jewel in its crown—the wine of kings and the king of wines. Made in the Tokaj region of the Northern Uplands, it uses native Furmint and Hárslevelü grapes and ranges from the pale, dry Tokaji Furmint to the rich amber Tokaji aszú dessert wine. The latter is one of the world's great sweet wines and has had its praises sung by Louis XIV, Beethoven, Schubert and Robert Browning—even Sherlock Holmes is known to have enjoyed the odd glass now and then. Its degree of sweetness is expressed in *puttonyos*, numbered from 3 to 6 (the sweetest) and indicating the quantity of baskets *(puttony)* of "noble" grapes added to each barrel of wine.

More popularly identified with Hungary is Bull's Blood from around Eger (Egri Bikavér), a red table wine whose name tells you all you need to know about its full-bodied character. It is a compound of four types of grapes. It goes perfectly with Hungary's abundance of meaty dishes, as do the younger reds, Kékfrankos and Kékoportó, and the fine Villányi-Burgundi.

But most of the country's wines are white. To accompany Lake Balaton fish, you should try a Lake Balaton wine. The Romans, who first brought wine-growing techniques to Hungary, loved the wines made here. From the vineyards around Badacsony, on the lake's north shore, look out for a range of white wines using well-known grape varieties, including the Olaszrízling, a medium-bodied Riesling, Traminer and Pinot Blanc.

The Tisza

Originating in the Carpathian mountains of western Ukraine, the Tisza winds slowly through Hungary southwards and finally links up with the Danube in Serbia, just north of Belgrade. It actually flows longer inside Hungary than the Danube. Notorious for flooding, it has been improved by the construction of thousands of kilometres of embankments, straightened out in places and harnessed to provide hydroelectric power and irrigation. The best-known cities along its shores are Tokaj, in the northeast region of Hungary, and Szeged in the south. Both have gastronomic connections, Tokaj for its fine wines, Szeged for spicy salami and a highly seasoned fish soup.

Tokaj lies at the spot where the Tisza makes a 90° turn southwards, at a conjunction with the scenic Bodrog river. Terraced vineyards cling to the hillside above town; the streets are full of wine cellars where you can taste many varieties of their sweet wines. One cellar has been converted into a museum *(Tokaji múzeum)* documenting the ancient methods of production.

Szeged is a river port and cultural centre, boasting two universities which confer on the city a young and cheerful atmosphere. The layout of concentric boulevards and streets on a grid pattern was devised after a devastating flood in 1879, when the city was virtually swept away. Most of the buildings are modern. In the town centre on Széchenyi tér, among lawns, flower gardens and fountains, the ornate City Hall, in what is known as Eclectic baroque style, was built after the flood, each floor with its own style of window. South from here is the main shopping area, reserved for pedestrians. The great pinnacled Votive Church *(Fogadalmi templom),* with eight clocks on its twin towers, was erected as a memorial after the flood, with construction beginning in 1913. The Szeged Summer Festival of opera and ballet is held in the square outside. Nearby is the medieval Tower of St Demetrius, sturdy enough to have resisted destruction. An 18th-century Serbian church boasts a superb collection of Orthodox icons.

By the river at the Palace of Education and Culture, the Ferenc Móra Museum gives insight into Szeged's history, with reproductions of peasants' living quarters, Hun and Avar handicrafts, and documents the importance of the River Tisza. 29

Croatia and Serbia

After leaving Hungary, the Danube serves as a frontier between Croatia and Serbia, and is no longer called *Duna*, but *Dunav*.

At **Kopacki Rit** near Osijek, there's an extensive ornithological reserve—the largest in Europe, excepting the Danube Delta.

The Veliki-Bački Canal begins in Serbia at **Bezdan** (km 1425), the border station. Linking the Danube and one of its major tributaries, the Tisza, this 123-km (76-mile) link was built in 1801 but has now lost its economic importance. The Banat, a fertile plain bounded by the Danube and Tisza, was settled by Swabians from Germany after the Turks were driven out. Incidentally, many of the German immigrants found jobs on Danube ships.

German settlers also founded **Apatin** (km 1401) in the 18th century, though only a small proportion of the population is German nowadays. The town gained fame for its hemp ropes and beer.

At km 1382 the Croatian Drava flows into the Danube, greatly increasing the volume of water and diverting the course of the river. In this stretch, the

Danube snakes around madly, creating a multitude of islands, side branches and shallows that tax a little on the ships' captains navigational skills.

The handsome buildings and picturesque courtyards of the historic centre of **Vukovar** (km 1333) unfortunately suffered severe damage in 1991 during the civil war in former Yugoslavia, but after its reconstruction the city will no doubt once more become a favourite port of call for Danube cruise ships.

The town of **Ilok** (km 1299) on the right bank dates from Roman times; in the Middle Ages it was one of the strongest fortresses on the Danube. Thanks to its picturesque situation above the river, its walls and castle, which today houses a Franciscan monastery, the town is completely charming. On the opposite bank in Serbia lies the important agricultural centre of **Bačka Palanka**.

As you coast along the river you'll pass countless villages with houses typical of the time of the Danube Swabians. Grapes and plums flourish on the wooded slopes of the **Fruška Gora** stretching along the right bank. There are seventeen ancient monasteries in these hills, belonging to the Serb

Orthodox Church. The whole area has been designated a nature reserve.

Then you will sail into **Novi Sad** (km 1255), the principal town of Vojvodina, the granary of former Yugoslavia. The town was founded at the end of the 17th century by Serbs fleeing from the Turks. In 1748 Novi Sad was declared a royal free city; a century later the Hungarians virtually razed it to the ground. In the 19th century the town became a cultural and intellectual focus for the Serbs within the Austro-Hungarian empire, when it became known as (yet another) Athens of the North.

Architecturally, Novi Sad offers little of interest, but it does have a pleasant museum and an art gallery with an extensive collection of paintings.

In 1999 the three bridges of Novi Sad were destroyed by NATO bombs; since then they have all been replaced; the last, the Sloboda (Liberty) Bridge, completed in 2005.

RAIN DANCE

The Indians of North America are not the only ones who perform dances to pray for rain: similar customs have also been known on the Danube. In Serbia's Bačka Palanka, men and women would dance at the harvest festival, douse each other with water and sing for the heavens to open. A group of girls would proceed through the village, their leader clad only in flowers, grass and leaves, to be greeted from each threshold with a bucketful of water…

Standing opposite the town on the right bank of the river, the fortress of **Petrovaradin** is well worth a visit—take a look at the clock tower: the hour hand is longer than the minute hand. Fortified by monks in the 13th century, the citadel fell to Suleiman the Magnificent three centuries later. Prince Eugène of Savoy—celebrated in folk songs as the "noble knight"—managed to drive out the Turks in 1716. The Austrians undertook construction of a new citadel, using plans drawn up by the famous French military architect Vauban. As Napoleon's armies advanced upon Vienna, the treasures of the Imperial Court were hurried to the safety of Petrovaradin. In the mid-19th century, Hungarian freedom fighters captured the fortress, but they were overcome by loyalist Croats and Serbs. For a long time afterwards the citadel served as both barracks and prison, housing such illustrious inmates as Josip Broz, later to become Marshal Tito.

Continuing downriver you reach **Sremski Karlovci** (km 1244), a pretty little town with fine baroque houses. It's famous in history as the place where the peace treaty of 1699 (the Treaty of Karlowitz) was signed by Austria, Turkey, Poland and Venice, putting an end to the war against the Turks and giving Austria supremacy in the Balkans. Apparently the room in which the treaty was signed had to be provided with four doors, as the delegations couldn't come to an agreement as to which of them was to enter first.

33

To return to the present, Sremski Karlovci is also known for its excellent red wine (and also its rosé); the best place to sample them is right here on the spot.

The stronghold of **Stari Slankamen** (km 1215) is a reminder of a battle against the Ottomans in 1691; today's visitors come for a peaceful soak in the warm, sodium-rich waters of the geothermal springs.

A little further downstream, the **River Tisza** ends its long journey from the Carpathians and across the Great Hungarian Plain (Nagy Alföld) by entering the Danube, where it considerably increases the volume of water. With a length of 977 km (607 miles), of which about half are navigable, the Tisza is the Danube's longest tributary. Some cruises make sidetrips up the Tisza as far as Tokaj in Hungary (see p. 29).

Zemun (km 1173), now just a suburb of Belgrade, was founded by the Romans, who called it Taurunum. After 1526 the Turks fortified the town; later it fell to Austria, and until 1918 the Hungarian border ran past here.

The ruins of Golubac castle in Serbia; it was held by the Turks for 260 years.

The capital of Serbia, **Belgrade** (Beograd; km 1170) lies on the confluence of Danube and Sava. You won't see many old buildings here, and no wonder, as the city has been destroyed no less than 20 times. Since the end of World War II it has changed from a small Balkan town to a European metropolis with an emphasis on building up the scientific, educational, cultural and conference infrastructure. However, the fortress—another masterpiece by Vauban—still commands respect from its setting in a pretty park,Kalemegdan, on the hilltop overlooking the mouth of the Sava.

Fed by numerous tributaries on its way to the Black Sea, the Danube below Belgrade swells to almost 1500 m (1640 yd), which makes it Europe's widest river. It now flows through fertile plains towards the Carpathians. Citadels and fortresses dotted along the banks bear witness to a turbulent history. The fortress of **Smederevo** or Semendria (km 1116), for example, was coveted and fought over by various powers. It was built by the Serbian despot Djuradj Brankovič in 1430, only to be captured by the Ottomans in 1459. The historic fortification was badly damaged by the bombardments of World War II, but

still seems to stand in proud defiance of all foes. Branković's cruel wife Jerina, who forced the people of the town to build the fortress despite fearful sacrifices, lives on in Serbian folktales.

At Ram, before the border between Serbia and Romania, stands another small castle, **Ramski Grad** (km 1075), built by the Turks but subsequently held by many different powers.

Serbia and Romania

As the Danube leaves the Pannonian Basin, the Southern Carpathians loom closer. Below **Moldova Veche** (km 1048, on the site of the Roman settlement of Mudava), there begins a 130-km (80-mile) stretch of rapids and cataracts through the narrow defile of the so-called Iron Gate, the terror of sailors in bygone days. The raging torrent has been tamed by construction of a hydroelectric plant, and

---

CRIME AND PUNISHMENT AT THE IRON GATE

It's said that a Turkish aga once kept a harem in the castle of Golubac. When he discovered that one of his most beautiful wives had run off with a Hungarian nobleman, he had the seducer captured and beheaded, bound the severed head to the hair of his errant wife, and chained the unfortunate girl to a rock in the middle of the Danube. To this day it has retained the name of Babakai (Turkish for "Repent!"). According to a less gory version, the girl escaped, but the vengeful aga fell in battle against the Christians.

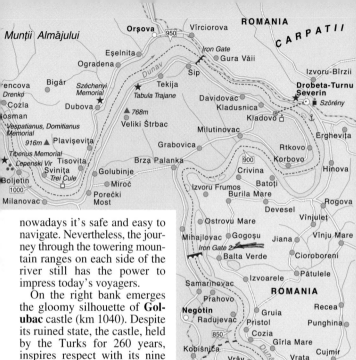

nowadays it's safe and easy to navigate. Nevertheless, the journey through the towering mountain ranges on each side of the river still has the power to impress today's voyagers.

On the right bank emerges the gloomy silhouette of **Golubac** castle (km 1040). Despite its ruined state, the castle, held by the Turks for 260 years, inspires respect with its nine massive towers joined by a ring of walls. The **Babakai** rock rises steeply from the depths of the river. A compelling picture which cannot help but inspire myths and legends.

The settlement of **Lepenski Vir** (km 1004) dates back to 8000–4000 BC but was not discovered until 1965. To protect it, archeologists transferred the buildings to higher ground on a hill above the river.

The complex ground plans of the excavated buildings testify to a high level of cultural development, and the large river pebbles which were found on this spot, carved with fishlike faces, are the earliest sculptures of this sort discovered in Europe.

As you advance along the river, the walls of rock close in, becoming ever steeper. In the gorges of Upper and Lower Kazan (km 974–965), the Danube narrows to a width of only 150 m (164 yd).

On the right bank, look out for the weathered marble **Tabula Trajana** (Trajan's Plaque; km 964) set here in AD 101 in honour of the Roman emperor. In a few unpretentious words, it commemorates construction of Trajan's Road along the Danube, a great feat for the time. The plaque was actually moved a little further up the bank from its original position when the reservoir was built.

Unfortunately nothing was done to save the old town of **Orsova**, which dated back to the Roman settlement of Tierna, the end point of Trajan's Road. It disappeared beneath the waters when the river was dammed. A modern port with the same name (km 955) was built higher up on the right bank, where the river opens into a wide bay.

From here you can make an interesting side-trip to the nearby spa of **Băile Herculane** (Baths of Hercules) in the nar-

---

THE IRON GATE

Just after entering Romania, the Danube flows into a narrow defile, 135 km (84 miles) long, separating the Carpathian Mountains from the Balkans and known as the Iron Gate. In some places, the sheer rock walls on each side of the river stretch to a height of over 700 m (2,297 ft). Once feared for its rapids and falls, the Iron Gate was opened to large ships after the inauguration of the gigantic Djerdap hydroelectric power station in 1971, shared between Romania and Serbia.

The dam provides a considerable quantity of power for the two countries but caused the disappearance of several towns, which were submerged by the waters. The other victims were sturgeons, who can no longer swim upstream to lay their eggs. At Drobeta-Turnu-Severin you can see the remains of Trajan's bridge, built in 105 on the orders of the Emperor by the Greek architect Apollodorus of Damascus and depicted on Trajan's Column in Rome.

row Cerna valley. These hot sulphurous springs (over 40 °C) set amidst delightful country-side have lost nothing of the popularity they used to enjoy in Roman times. In the 19th century the spa resort was frequented by a wealthy clientèle mainly made up of members of the Austro-Hungarian bourgeoisie. Franz-Joseph and his wife each had their own pavilion. People came to cure rheumatism, as well as nervous and digestive problems. In winter, you can ski on neighbouring slopes.

The island of **Ada Kaleh** (km 952) suffered the same fate as ancient Orsova and Trajan's Road when the reservoir was built for the hydroelectric plant at the Iron Gate. A fragment of the Orient in the middle of the Danubian region was lost for ever here—its Turkish coffee houses, bazaars, picturesque alleys and gardens, and its characteristic atmosphere are submerged for ever beneath the river. Attempts were made to rescue a few buildings on Simi-an island further downstream (km 927).

To pass the **Iron Gate** in the old days, your ship would have been towed by locomotive and tug along a canal to avoid the danger spot. Construction of the Yugoslav-Romanian Djerdap Power Station in 1971 may have changed the riverscape greatly, but at least ships can now sail cheerfully through. But unsuspected victims were the sturgeons which used to swim upstream from the Black Sea.

The ancient Dacian settlement of **Drobeta-Turnu Severin** (km 931) takes you far back from the achievements of the 20th century. Under orders from Trajan, architect Apollodorus of Damascus built a bridge across the Danube here in AD 105; some of its piers have survived to the present day. The bridge was demolished under Hadrian, Trajan's successor, but you can still see it what it looked like whole if you take a trip to Rome and examine the reliefs on Trajan's Column. It shows the high level of sophistication the Dacian civilization had attained, such as villages with timber houses, linen clothing with Thracian-style trousers.

Today's Turnu Severin is a major port. In Rose Park, statues commemorate Trajan and his rival, the Dacian king Decebalus. Remains of a medieval fortification date from the days when the Crusaders set off from here for Asia Minor. The Municipal Museum provides a fascinating glimpse of the town's history with a rich archeological and ethnographic collection.

Romania and Bulgaria

The mouth of the River Timok (km 846) marks the border between Serbia and Bulgaria. The Danube flows majestically through the great plain of **Walachia**. For the next 470 km (290 miles), the river forms the frontier between Romania and Bulgaria. On the Romanian bank, the *Dunărea* flows past flat lands studded with reed-fringed lakes, whilst the Bulgarian bank of the *Dunav* is often steep and rocky. As the river used to burst its banks here frequently in former times, no one risked building villages by the water's edge.

Almost opposite **Calafat** (km 795), once a fortified city and now an industrial centre, lies the town of **Vidin** (km 790), one of the most ancient in Bulgaria. Both Celts and Thracians valued this favourable location on the Danube, and the Romans built the fortress of Bononia here, destroyed several times by the Huns and Avars. The town's heyday was in the 14th century when, under the name of Bdin, it was capital of the principality of the same name. But it fell to the Ottomans in 1396. The Turkish feudal lord Osman Pasvantooglu took it as his own personal fief from 1793 to 1807.

Stretch your legs in the park and long, shady promenade along the Danube. If you visit the town be sure to see the interesting mosque and mausoleum-like library (c. 1800) of Osman Pasvantooglu, who rebelled against the Sultan. The mosque is built in typical oriental style

but instead of the crescent moon that normally tops the dome, here it is an arrow-head—eloquent testimony to its builder's insubordination.

The impressive fortress of Baba Vida, directly on the river bank in the north part of the park, dates back to the 10th century and was extended and strengthened in the 14th century. Today it serves as backdrop for theatrical performances.

Lom (km 734) was also built on the site of a Roman fortification, called Almus. Finds from Roman times can be seen in the town's museum. Today, Lom is Bulgaria's second-largest Danube port, after Ruse.

On the Romanian side, the river flows past a long stretch of lakes, teeming with fish.

The next Bulgarian town of importance is **Kozloduj** (km 700), the site of a dramatic incident in 1876. The 28-year-old Bulgarian poet and freedom fighter Christo Botev forced the captain of the Danube steamer *Radetzky* to moor here, so that he and his 200 followers could take up the fight against the Turks. Shortly afterwards he and his comrades-in-arms lost their lives, but to this day their act of bravery is commemorated by bouquets of flowers laid prominently on the river bank, spelling out Botev's initials in Cyrillic script. The episode was also immortalized in a popular folk song.

High up in a picturesque landscape of cornfields and vineyards, the town of **Orjahovo** (km 678) is an agricultural centre.

At km 641, the **Three Generations Memorial** was set up to

commemorate three Bulgarian wars of independence.

Near to the small port of Bajkal at the mouth of the Iskar (km 636), important finds from Roman times were unearthed at **Gigen**. The foundations of a large temple, precious mosaics, paved streets, water mains and sewers indicate that this was the site of the Roman town of Ulpius Escus.

Nikopol (km 597) also looks back to a Roman past. Trajan achieved a major victory over the Dacians here and named the fort "Town of the Victory on the Lower Danube" *(Nicopolis ad Istrum)*. In 629 the Byzantine Emperor Heraclius had the fortress extended. The Turks strengthened it further, but in 1810 the Russians pulled down the massive fortifications. The ruins are still worth a visit, and you might also like to peep into the small 13th-century church nearby.

From here you can take an overland trip to **Pleven**, the biggest and most important town on the Danube plain—and one of the most ancient. It was settled in prehistoric times (4th to 3rd millennium BC), and then variously held, much later, by the Thracians, Romans, Slavs and Turks. Several churches are worth a visit, as are the History Museum and Skobelev Park, where the historic battle for Pleven (1877), which played a central role in Bulgaria's fight for independence against the Turks, is depicted realistically in a circular panorama.

The mausoleum in the city centre commemorates the Russian and Romanian troops who fell in 1877.

At **Svištov** (km 554) the Danube approaches its most southerly point. The town's terraced layout on the hilly banks above the river gives it particular charm. Among the sights in this major port are two unusual 17th-century underground churches, as well as the Holy Trinity Church and the museum dedicated to the Bulgarian writer Konstantinov, murdered at the age of 34.

Ruse (km 495) is Bulgaria's fourth largest city and the country's biggest Danube port. Back when the Roman fleet was stationed here, the place was called Sextanta Prista ("Sixty Ships"). A new settlement under the name of Ruse is first mentioned at the beginning of the 16th century; the Turks later named it Ruschuk. In the 19th century the city experienced an upturn in its fortunes: the first railway in the Ottoman Empire (from Ruschuk to Varna on the Black Sea) was opened here.

Little of historical interest has survived. The neo-baroque buildings in the city centre confer on Ruse the appearance of an old Austrian provincial town. Sights include the Holy Trinity Church (Sveta Troiza) of 1764 with its beautiful icons and frescoes, and the National Theatre (1891). Outside the centre, the railway station is the largest and conidered the finest in the country. Opposite the Hotel Riga, the local History and Lifestyle Museum occupies a handsome wooden house.

For rest and recreation, the inhabitants of this industrial town have many parks to choose from, as well as the Lipnik Nature Reserve 12 km (7.5 miles)

ORTHODOX CHURCH

Following a succession of conflicts between the 9th and 11th century, the Eastern Church with its Byzantine rituals broke away from the Roman Church. As the beliefs of the East and West churches are very similar, the separation was recognized as the Great Schism, and not considered heretical. The Orthodox Church (from the Greek *orthos* "right, true" and *doxa* "meaning") consists of independent national churches governed by Patriarchs. The Russian Orthodox Church is the largest, followed by the Romanian. In Bulgaria, the Church has become increasingly popular since the changes of 1989 and the democratization of the country, and it has a great influence on everyday life.

away. Another worthwhile excursion is to the cliff monasteries of Ivanovo (12th–15th centuries) with their unique murals, listed by UNESCO.

The "Friendship Bridge"—an imposing metal construction, and Europe's second longest bridge at 2,224 m (2,433 yd)—takes you across the river to the Romanian town of **Giurgiu** (km 493). The name originates from Genoese sailors who built a trading station and a castle, San Giorgio, here in the 14th century. Of the great Turkish fortress only a lopsided watchtower in the town centre remains.

However, most people disembarking in Giurgiu don't spend long in the town, but head off instead for **Bucharest** 64 km (40 miles) inland. The Romanian capital, once styled the "Paris of the East", was much

mangled by Ceausescu's architectural tastes, and since his demise it is struggling to find a sense of balance. It is well worth seeing for its museums and churches, its jolting juxtaposition of grandeur and poverty, and above all for the lively, friendly character of the people, renowned for their cheerful outlook on life and who seem to thrive in face of adversity.

Further downstream at km 432/430, two towns again face each other on the banks of the river: Bulgarian **Tutrakan**, an important fishing centre, and Romanian **Oltenița** with a major shipyard. Both settlements existed back in Roman times. Inland from Tutrakan you come to **Ezero Srebarna**, a 15 sq km (6 sq mile) lake which is home to rare birds like ibises and pelicans.

Silistra (km 375), only a few hundred metres from the Bulgarian-Romanian border, was founded by Trajan in the 2nd century AD. In 1942 a Roman tomb was discovered here with very beautiful, well-preserved mural paintings from the 4th century, depicting scenes of family life, hunting, plants and birds. The old Turkish fortress of Silistra has also resisted the ravages of time.

Northwards and into Ukraine

On the right bank begins the **Dobrogea** plateau, stretching all the way to the Black Sea; the Baragan plain on the left bank is reminiscent of the Hungarian puszta. The bygone romanticism of this steppe landscape

has been captured in the books of the Romanian writer Panait Istrati.

At km 370 the Danube splits into two branches, the narrower Borcea branch and the main river. A ferry from Călăraşi crosses the Braţul Borcea to Ostrov. From here, the road snakes through a beautiful area to Adamclisi, where a Roman memorial, the **Tropaeum Trajani**, commemorates Trajan's momentous victory over the Dacians. The road continues through the vineyards of Murfatlar, which produce a sweet white dessert wine of the same name, to reach Constanţa, Romania's biggest port on the Black Sea. This is also the terminus of the 64-km (40-mile) Danube Canal, completed in 1983.

Back to the river. In **Cernavodă** (km 300), which means "Black Water", the Danube is at its closest to the Black Sea. The Danube Canal starts here. Another great feat of engineering is the railway bridge, built in 1895 and a significant aid in the economical development of the Danubian region.

After Cernavodă the river turns northwards. On the right bank, **Ghindăreşti** (km 260) comes into view, a small, old Russian fishing village in a very picturesque location. The domes of the Orthodox church have a silvery gleam.

Like most places on the lower Danube, **Hîrşova** (km 253) was a Roman camp and later a Turkish fortress. The fine Russian Orthodox church was founded by the Lipovani sect, which is now mainly to be found in the delta. Today a bridge spans the river; in earlier times, shepherds from Transylvania crossed here to graze their flocks on the fertile Dobrogea plain.

Here the river again splits into two branches, embracing a 60-km (37-mile) reed-covered island and reuniting at **Brăila** (km 170). This port, which was first mentioned in 1368, was fought over fiercely in the Middle Ages. It was defended by a Turkish fortress for almost 300 years, finally pulled down in 1829. Today Brăila is home to various industries; the reeds from the Danube delta are processed here. Brăila is the birthplace of the Romanian writer Panait Istrati (1884–1935), son of a laundress and a Greek smuggler. He published in French; his best-known work is *The Confession of a Loser*.

At **Galaţi** (km 150), between the mouths of two large tributaries, the Danube makes its last decisive turn to the east. The town was founded 500 years ago but it doesn't look its age,

for heavy damage in World War II left nothing of the old centre. As in Brăila, all life centres round the harbour, which has a large shipyard.

Downriver (km 134), the Prut, the second-longest tributary, flows into the Danube. This is also the border between Romania and Ukraine. The next sizeable town, **Reni** (km 128), is an important Ukrainian commercial port.

On the right bank you will pass by the former Turkish fortress of **Isaccea** (km 102). Its name derives from Turkish *Isak-Kioi* ("Isaac's Village"). Honey is harvested from bees that feed in the extensive linden woodlands of the region; tobacco cultivation, wine making and fishing are other important sources of income.

The Delta

Now the landscape along the river changes markedly: at km 80 the delta begins. The "King of European Rivers" (as Napoleon once called it) has reached its goal, emptying slowly and majestically into the Black Sea.

The Danube delta is a world apart. To this day, no road crosses this watery kingdom, and the only way to explore the streams, the waterlily-carpeted lakes and the lonely fishing villages is by boat. Tulcea and Vilkovo are the usual starting points for excursions into the delta to explore its flora and fauna, unique in Europe.

In the delta, the Danube splits into three main branches: to the north the Chilia, in the middle the canalized Sulina branch, the

WOODWORK

Wood plays an important part in the arts and crafts of many country districts in Romania. The thick forests, the little means and difficulties of transport have helped the architects and artisans develop unique skills. In the Maramureş, most of the buildings are made of wood. Houses, mills, wells, churches, all were constructed of wood without the use of a single nail, the beams and flooring all dovetailed together. Ox-carts, furniture, household utensils and many other every-day objects are still made from wood, often carefully carved into intricate patterns. Everything from house doors to dowry chests and wooden spoons are decorated with flowers, animals and twisted rope designs, symbolizing the thread of life.

Rustic textiles and rugs are also attractive and hard-wearing; embroidered with flowers or woven in geometric patterns, predominantly red and white.

main thoroughfare for shipping traffic, and in the south the Sfântu Gheorghe branch, the oldest and least spoilt, and where it spreads out into a vast delta shared between Romania (82%) and Ukraine. With the immense lagoons of Razelm and Sinoe, it covers some 5,165 sq km (over 1900 sq miles), of which half are protected as a Biosphere Reserve.

The silt carried by the current has created a labyrinth of arms, nearly 400 lakes, spongy islands *(plauri),* meadows and dunes

linked by a vast network of canals. In some places you'll see elevated *grinds,* plateaux formed by deposits where trees have taken root. Reeds are everywhere and serve a useful purpose: they filter the polluted waters upstream.

A transition between the earth, the river and the sea, the immense delta, at the confluence of five migratory routes, is also the refuge of some 280 species of bird. In the marshes, there are eight different members of the heron family alone,

including grey, purple and great white herons, little egrets and bitterns, as well as Dalmatian and white pelicans, storks, ibises, spoonbills and white-tailed eagles. Cormorants perch on the bank, drying their wings.

The land-based fauna include wildcats, wolves, wild boar, foxes and otters.

The waters teem with fish, which form the staple diet of the human and animal inhabitants: pike, carp, pike-perch, catfish, tench, perch and bream, and sturgeon regularly swim up from the Black Sea. But freshwater herring are the fisherman's most important catch.

The 15,000 inhabitants of the delta live mostly from collecting reeds, fish farming and traditional fishing. In majority they are Lipovani, Russian Old Believers who fled here in the 17th century in the face of persecution by the Orthodox Church. Their churches often hold precious icons of limewood (*lipa* in Russian), and their traditional costumes and customs give the visitor a vivid impression of life in old Russia.

Here and there, you will see tiny villages of reed-thatched houses, blending in perfectly with their surroundings and accessible only by boat. For several days each spring, the river floods, seeping through the doorways and carrying away stabilized lands.

In the small town of **Tulcea** (km 71), "Gateway to the Delta", you can get a good overview of the local flora and fauna in the Danube Delta Museum. The town was built on the site of a Roman settlement, Aegissus. It is a significant port and industrial centre, with no particular charm, but the harbour bustles with luxury boats taking visitors on trips into the delta.

Downstream from Tulcea, passenger boats ply back and forth between fishing craft and rusting cargoes along the 64 km (38 miles) of the Sulina branch, channelled and deepened to allow the passage of large ships in the 1869s. Merchandise and passengers are unloaded at regular intervals in the little villages scattered along the banks.

Via **Crişan**, one of the largest fishing villages in the delta, you reach the port of **Sulina**, where the Danube flows into the Black Sea. Already a settlement in Byzantine times, Sulina was later a mooring point for Genoese ships. Since the 19th-century, this former fishing village has developed shipyards and a fish-processing industry. Here, the work of the river is highlighted: by depositing 80 million tons of silt and gaining 40 m from the sea each year, it has

moved the lighthouse from the shore to the middle of the marketplace!

Sfântu Gheorghe is the capital of the sturgeon fishermen at the mouth of the southernmost and oldet of the three branches.

The northernmost branch, **Chilia**, is in places over 1000 m wide. Alone it carries two thirds of the river waters to the delta. It is longer (120 km, 74 miles) and more tortuous than the others, and dotted with little islands, and was long ignored because it marked the boundary with the Soviet Union. At its mouth, it breaks up into myriad mini-deltas. At km 90 lies **Izmail**. The earliest settlers here were probably Scythians, followed later by Greeks, Romans and Slavs. From the 15th century onwards, the fortress was the focus of bitter fighting between the Russians and Turks. In 1790 the Russian generals Suvorov and Kutusov succeeded in capturing the town, but Izmail was not to become completely Russian until 1870. Suvorov is commemorated by an equestrian statue and a museum. **Vilkovo** (km 15), the "Ukrainian Venice", was founded in the 18th century by Cossacks.

SONS OF THE DANUBE

Two 20th-century writers, both famous for works written in a language other than their mother tongue, were born on the lower Danube.

Panait Istrati was the son of a Greek smuggler in Brăila. He led an adventurous life and celebrated the magic of the Baragan steppes and the banks of the Danube mostly in French, a language which he had taught himself.

Elias Canetti describes his birthplace, Ruse, which at that time still went by its Turkish name, in his autobiography: "Ruschuk [...] was a marvellous town [...], inhabited by people of the most varied origins; on any one day you could hear seven or eight languages spoken." In his childhood, the main languages were Spanish, his mother tongue, and Bulgarian; yet his books, for which he was awarded the Nobel Prize in 1981, were written in German.

LINZ

Musical City

Capital of the province of Upper Austria, Linz rises from the banks of the Danube at an important communications junction with Germany and the Czech Republic. The river accounts in good measure for the city's prosperity, since transport is crucial to its mining, metallurgical and chemical industries. Perhaps because of its industrial image, Linz has been somewhat neglected by the tourist. Yet it is full of delights, including a handsome, well-preserved Old Town with elegant 17th- and 18th-century buildings, a castle and many lovely old churches. In the past, countless scholars, poets, musicians and architects found the town a most congenial place to put down roots: astronomer Johannes Kepler taught at the university in the 17th century; Anton Bruckner was organist at the cathedral in the 19th century; Mozart and Beethoven stopped here long enough to write the Linz Symphony and the 8th respectively.

A BRIEF HISTORY	
Roman times	Romans settle at this site commanding the Danube and the ancient salt route from Hallstatt to Bohemia, calling it Lentia.
Medieval times	Thanks to the Danube transport, crucial to Linz's iron and wood industries, the town prospers.
15th–18th centuries	Friedrich III makes Linz a regional capital of the Holy Roman Empire in 1490, and in 1497 builds the first bridge over the Danube between Passau and Vienna. From the 16th century Linz plays host to many writers, musicians, scholars. In 1785 the town becomes a bishop's seat.
19th century	In 1832 the first (horsedrawn) railroad on the continent is inaugurated in Linz, running to Budweis in Bohemia, and five years later the first Danube steamship calls, encouraging the buildup of machine industries and textiles.
20th century– present	The town is badly bombed by the Allies in 1945. Postwar, the city concentrates on heavy industry and chemicals. In the 1990s and congress and trade fair centre are built, as well as the Ars Electronica Center, using state-of-the-art techniques of virtual reality.

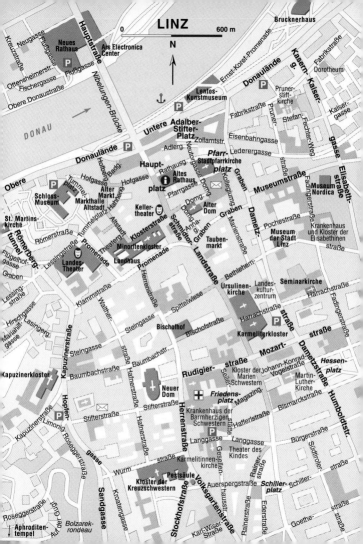

Sightseeing

The heart of the remarkably well-preserved Old Town *(Altstadt)* on Linz's south bank centres around the **Hauptplatz**, with its stately pastel-coloured buildings from the 17th and 18th centuries and an imposing Gothic city hall. The magnificent Baroque cathedral *(Alter Dom)* is where the composer Anton Bruckner served as organist (1824–96). In the middle of the square juts the tall white-marble Trinity Column of thanksgiving erected in 1723. Indeed there was much to be thankful for: the town had just recovered from a Turkish invasion, a fire and the plague. A carillon plays music of Austrian composers in the square several times a day.

The **Landhaus**, a few steps away, is a gracious Renaissance palace with arcaded courtyard and flower-bedecked balconies. Its fountain depicts the planets, recalling that the great German astronomer Kepler taught in this building in the 17th century, when it was a university. Today it houses the provincial government and is a popular venue for concerts.

The ancient **castle** on the Danube, one of the residences of the Emperor Friedrich III, is now the Landesmuseum. Displays cover the history of Upper Austria through the ages, illustrated with arms, handicrafts and local art. Nearby **St Martin church** existed already in the time of Charlemagne; it is conserved in its original state.

To most conveniently see these Old Town sights, board one of the miniature trains leaving on the hour from the Hauptplatz. Be sure to return in the evening, as it is a lively place for nightlife.

One reason to cross the river is to take the steep train that goes up the Pöstlingberg, providing a view over the town.

On Linz's doorstep is one of the world's most magnificent Baroque edifices, the **Abbey St Florian**, 18 km (10 miles) to the southeast. Augustinian monks lived here as early as the 11th century, but the buildings were remodelled (completed 1751) by Italian Carlo Carlone and Austrian Jakob Prandtauer, the architect of Melk monastery further down the Danube. Anton Bruckner, Austria's greatest composer of religious music in the 19th century and former choirboy at St Florian, is buried in the crypt under the great organ he loved to play. Nearby, the Palladian-style **Schloss Hohenbrunn**, built by Jakob Prandtauer, was completed in 1732 for the prior of St Florian.

SALZBURG

The Sound of Music

A golden city, home of Mozart and a thousand other musical dreams, Salzburg lies in an unequalled environment of mountains, hills and forest, along the banks of the River Salzach.

There is something indescribably southern about the old part of town, which many like to compare with Florence or Venice. Baroque architecture gives it a dreamy, poetic charm. Narrow streets lead into spacious squares, elegant settings for Gothic churches and monasteries and ornately sculpted fountains. Mansions and Renaissance palaces reign over beautiful parks and gardens. It is easy to imagine how the drama and lyricism of these ancient stones, this unique combination of Italianate and Germanic, should have influenced the music of one of the world's greatest composers. Today Salzburg is entirely pervaded by Mozart. Recitals are held in the most splendid ceremonial rooms of those palaces and castles; his homes are preserved as museums. There's the Mozarteum music academy, the annual festival, and even chocolates, Mozartkugeln, with his bewigged portrait on the red and gold wrapper.

Three prince-archbishops of the Renaissance modelled Salzburg, unspoiled even to this day. The Old Town is squeezed between the left bank of the river and a high ridge, the Mönchsberg. On top of this stands the impregnable fortress of Hohensalzburg, which has protected the city for more than 900 years. The more modern town spreads over the right bank, at the foot of a wooded hill, the Kapuzinerberg (638 m).

The city, with a population of 146,000, is capital of a federal state covering more than 8 per cent of the country's total area. Salzburger Land, as it is known, is renowned for its mountains, lakes, spas and castles. East of Salzburg begins the mineral-rich Salzkammergut, centred on Bad Ischl and popular for winter sports. Following the Salzach river valley south of the capital, a scenic road takes you to Hallein and the Dürrnberg salt mines, then the ice caves of the Eisriesenwelt. Excursions continue south along the Gastein Valley down to Kärnten (Carinthia), or to the southeast through the Tauerntunnel burrowing below the Radstädter Tauern range. Southwest of Salzburg, the Saalach valley crosses German territory at Berchtesgaden and sweeps down to Zell am Zee and the Grossglockner Highway, gateway to the Hohe Tauern National Park.

4th century BC– 5th century AD	Celts found a state with present-day Salzburg as capital and exploit the local salt mines. Taken over by the Romans in 14 BC and named Juvavum, the settlement prospers thanks to its favourable position at the crossing of important trade routes. In 477 the town is destroyed by the Gothic chieftain Odoacer.
6th–9th centuries	Christianity is introduced to the region by Bavarians. The Bishop of Worms, St Rupert, settles in the ruins of Juvavum in 696 and founds St Peter's Abbey and a Benedictine convent. The name Salzburg (Castle of Salt) appears in 755. The Irish bishop, St Virgil, founds the cathedral in 767. Salzburg becomes an archbishopric in 798.
10th century	A time of troubles, marked by Magyar raids.
11th–12th centuries	The fortress of Hohensalzburg is built in 1077. Friedrich Barbarossa burns down the town in 1167. It is rebuilt, with a new cathedral.
13th century	The town prospers. Archbishop Friedrich II is awarded the title Imperial Prince. Salzburg becomes one of the leading cities of the Holy Roman Empire.
14th–17th centuries	Wars with Bavaria in 1322 and Holy Roman Emperor Friedrich III in 1466, along with peasant revolt, do not hinder development of the city. The salt mines provide the main revenue of the prince-archbishops. Much of the city is destroyed by fire in 1598. It is rebuilt in Renaissance and baroque style by three archbishops, Wolf Dietrich von Raitenau, his cousin Marcus Sitticus, and Paris Lodron, who call in Italian architects Scamozzi and Soltari to redesign the city, cathedral and ramparts.
18th century	Wolfgang Amadeus Mozart is born in Salzburg in 1756 and lives there until 1781. In the Napoleonic Wars, Salzburg changes hands several times until it returns definitively to Austria in 1816.
19th century	Economic revival. In 1863 the railway reaches Salzburg. The music academy, the Mozarteum, is founded.
20th century– present	The Salzburg Festival is established in 1920. The town becomes popular with tourists. It celebrates Mozart's 250th birthday in 2006.

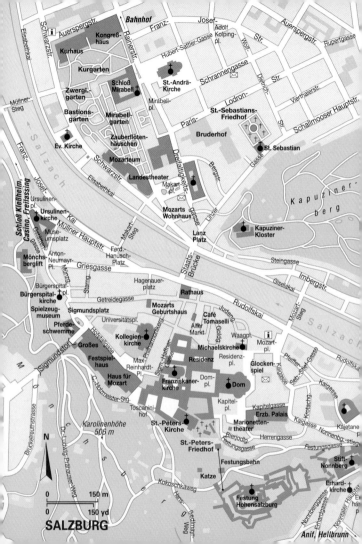

SALZBURG

Sightseeing

A good place to start exploring is the heart of the **Old Town** on the left bank of the river. In the centre of **Residenzplatz** stands a large baroque fountain (1658–61) surrounded by splendid rearing horses. At 7 and 11 a.m., and 6 p.m., familiar melodies by Mozart ring out on the 35 bells of the 17th-century **Glockenspiel**, on the east side of the square. The west side is taken up by the **Residenz**, an imposing palace of the archbishops founded in 1120 (the present buildings date from the 17th and 18th centuries). Guided tours take you through a succession of richly decorated ceremonial halls, antichambers and salons (*Prunkräume*), including the Conference Room where the young Mozart played in many a concert for the prince-archbishop and his guests. On the third floor, a suite of fifteen stuccoed chambers now serves as the **Residenzgalerie**, displaying works by great European painters from the 16th to 19th centuries.

The south side of Residenzplatz is dominated by the huge **Dom** (Cathedral), dedicated to St Rupert. It was built in Italian Renaissance style, with baroque overtones, between 1614 and 1655. In the first side chapel to the left of the entrance, is the Romanesque font, supported by four bronze lions, where baby Mozart was christened on January 28, 1756. Excavations of the medieval cathedral and Roman remains are displayed in the **Domgrabungsmuseum** (the entrance is under the north archway), while the cathedral treasury is presented in the **Dommuseum** inside the cathedral entrance, to the right.

The cathedral square (Domplatz) forms an enclosed courtyard; the **Mariensäule** (Virgin's Column) in the middle was sculpted by the Hagenauer brothers in the 1760s. Leaving Domplatz by the archway in the southeast corner, you reach **Kapitelplatz**, dominated by a white marble fountain (Kapitelschwemme) depicting Neptune. It was originally used for washing and watering horses. From the south side of this square, a road leads up to the lower station of the **Festungsbahn**, Austria's oldest cable railway (1892). It carries you up effortlessly in 90 seconds to **Hohensalzburg**, the sturdy archbishop's castle that watches over the city from a height of 120 m above the River Salzach. The castle was a fortress bristling with military defences, rather than a palatial retreat for spiritual meditation: the aristocratic 63

Salzburg archbishops were rarely popular enough to overcome the fear of civic rebellion. Guided tours visit the elegant 16th-century Princes' Rooms (*Fürstenzimmer*) in late-Gothic style, furnished by archbishop Leonhard von Keutschach (1495– 1519). One of the highlights is the Golden Hall (*Goldene Saal*), with wood panelled ceilings and ornate carving, not to be confused with the Golden Room (*Goldene Stube*) and its magnificent monumental ceramic tiled stove, each polychrome panel illustrating a scene from the Scriptures, flowers and fruit, coats of arms and portraits of local rulers. The **Burgmuseum** has a first-class collection of medieval sculpture; also on display are the weapons and instruments of torture used to bolster the archbishops' power, and objects illustrating everyday life in a medieval fortress. For the best view over the city's rooftops and domes, make your way to the **panoramic terrace** of the Kuenburg bastion, by a gateway to the right of St George's Church.

Back down at the bottom of Festungsgasse stands the **Stiftskirche St Peter** (St Peter's Church), first built from 1130 to 1143, altered in the early 17th century and richly remodelled in the rococo style with red and white Salzburg marble in the 1770s. Ceiling frescoes show scenes of the life of St Peter, by Johann Weiss of Augsburg. On the lower slopes of the Mönchsberg, the **cemetery**, shaded by pines and weeping willows, is the elegant, even romantic resting place of Salzburg's noblest families. Catacombs tunnelled into the rock are of early Christian origin.

Topped by a Gothic steeple, the **Franziskanerkirche**, a late-Romanesque convent church, was consecrated in 1223. The rather sober nave is lightened by the bright Gothic choir. The golden baroque high altar by the Viennese architect Johann Bernhard Fischer von Erlach frames a poignant 15th-century Madonna by the Tyrol's finest sculptor and painter, Michael Pacher. The Christ on her lap was added in 1895.

The **Rupertinum**, a 17th-century palace built by Paris Lodron, houses the museum of modern and contemporary art, with exhibitions of 20th-century painting, graphic art, sculpture and photography. Particularly noteworthy are the works by Kokoschka, Kirchner, Nolde and Egon Schiele.

Backing into the base of the Mönchsberg, the long building known as the **Festspielhaus** (Festival Hall) has been lovingly converted from the former court stables. It includes several theatres, the Haus für Mozart and other concert halls, and a riding school with three rows of seats carved out of the hillside. The 130 horses that were quartered in these palatial lodgings had the exclusive rights to the waters of the **Pferdeschwemme** on nearby Sigmundsplatz. A grandiose Renaissance structure of 1695, this horse trough to end all horse troughs is richly ornamented with frescoes of prancing steeds, dominated by a vigorous sculpted group by Michael Bernhard Mandl depicting a man breaking in a horse.

Next to the fountain, the **Neutor**, by the Hagenauer brothers, is the ornate entrance to a tunnel bored through the Mönchsberg in the 18th century to the western districts of Salzburg.

Opposite the Festival Hall, on the north side of Furtwängler Park, the **Kollegienkirche** (University Church, 1696–1707) figures among Fischer von Erlach's baroque masterpieces. The twin-towered convex façade presents an imposing frame for the massive dome looming behind it. The church looks onto **Universitätsplatz**, a long square surrounded by university buildings which is the site of a lively fruit, flower and vegetable market *(Grünmarkt)* every morning except Sunday.

Continuing to Museumsplatz at the northern end of the old town, you reach the **Haus der Natur**, a fascinating museum of natural history occupying no less than 80 rooms of a former Ursuline convent. Make sure you have plenty of time in hand to explore the collections of corals, the dinosaurs, the aquarium and reptile zoo, as well as the space discovery hall.

From nearby Gstättengasse, take the **lift** *(Mönchsbergaufzug)* up to the terrace of Café Winkler for another fabulous panoramic view over the city.

Back down at ground level, **Getreidegasse** is the great shopping street of Salzburg's old town. A veritable forest of wrought-iron guild signs ornament its Renaissance and baroque façades. The houses are narrow but four or five storeys high and delving deep on each side, around alleyways and hidden courtyards (at, for example, nos. 23, 25, 34 and 38). Number 9 is **Mozart's birthplace**—now an enchanting museum. Exhibits include manuscripts of minuets Mozart wrote when he was five, his counterpoint notebook, paintings of papa Leopold and sister Nannerl. A clavichord bears a note written by wife Constanze: "On this piano my dearly departed husband Mozart composed the Magic Flute".

Getreidegasse opens onto Rathausplatz; continue past the Town Hall to the **Alter Markt** on your right. Near the fountain, at no. 6, don't miss the delightful **pharmacy** (Hofapotheke) that has kept the rococo décor of the days when it was appointed to the prince-archbishops.

From the northeastern corner of Alter Markt, follow narrow Judengasse, one of the oldest and most picturesque streets in the town, to **Mozartplatz**, with a statue of Salzburg's favourite composer in the centre, by Ludwig Schwanthaler (1842).

Cross over to the right bank of the Salzach by the Mozartsteg bridge. From Steingasse, a long flight of stairs leads up to the Capuchin monastery that gives its name to **Kapuzinerberg**, built at the beginning of the 17th century.

Back down at river level, follow the bank downstream as far as Makartplatz. At No. 8, **Mozart's Residence**, also known as the Tanzmeisterhaus, was the family home from 1773 to 1780. It has been converted into a museum of musical instruments, and includes the **Ton- und Filmsammlung**, where you can consult any of 14,000 audio and 2000 video recordings.

Over to the right, **Trinity Church**, with a concave façade, is another of Fischer van Er-lach's baroque masterpieces (1694–1702).

The large building on the west side of the square is the State Theatre, with behind it the **Marionettentheater** where puppets perform *The Magic Flute*. Next door is the Mozarteum, the Academy of Music.

The seat of the local council, **Schloss Mirabell** was originally commissioned in 1606 by archbishop Wolf Dietrich von Raitenau for his mistress, Salome von Alt, and it became the summer residence of the prince-archbishops. After a fire in 1818 it was rebuilt by Peter de Nobile. A magnificent sculpted marble staircase surviving from the original palace leads to the gilded and stuccoed Marmorsaal, also original, where marriages are officiated today. The French-style formal gardens, by Fischer von Erlach, are peopled with statues of gods and goddesses. A staircase guarded by stone lions leads from the rose garden to a promenade on the ancient ramparts decorated with statues of dwarves—caricatures in marble of local worthies. The southern wing of the Orangerie houses a small **Baroque Museum**, displaying paintings, drawings and sculpture by artists of the 17th and 18th centuries, notably Bernini, Veronese, Tiepolo and Fragonard.

THE WACHAU

Land of Vines and Apricots

"The Wachau" is the name given to the delightful stretch of the Danube between Melk and Krems in Lower Austria (*Niederösterreich*). Just 30 km (19 miles) long, this belt of land basks in an exceptionally mild climate. Grapes and apricots (*Marillen* in Austrian German) flourish here, and the best way to enjoy them is to sample the delicious white wines, fiery apricot schnapps and rich abundance of cakes and desserts on offer in the local hostelries.

The name "Wachau" (formerly Wahowa) probably derived from *wacta* (watch-post on the river), or from the word *vahen,* to catch, as a reference to fishing.

Whatever your passion, the Wachau has something to offer: history buffs and adventurers can discover the castles from which robber barons used prey on merchant ships passing on the Danube; art lovers can marvel at the Benedictine abbey of Melk—a jewel of baroque architecture—and the lovely old town of Krems; connoisseurs of medieval legend and literature can follow in the footsteps of the Nibelungs; people interested in folklore can rediscover old legends and customs—and the rest of us can just relax and enjoy the magical setting and make explorations into the realms of the hearty Lower Austrian cooking.

The Wachau is easily accessible from Vienna by car—90 km (56 miles) on the motorway, or by Danube steamship. Until 1972, when a bridge was built over the Danube near Melk, the only way to cross the river was by ferry. The best times to see this fascinating region are spring and autumn when the weather is mild and it is not too crowded.

A BRIEF HISTORY	
Prehistory	Archeological finds, such as the "Galgenberg Dancing Venus" and the "Willendorf Venus", prove that the Wachau was already inhabited in the Paleolithic.
1st century BC	The Danube forms the northern border of the Roman Empire. The Romans make improvements to viniculture, introduced to the Wachau by the Celts.
4th century AD	Goths, Huns and Avars from the Asian steppes invade the Danube basin.

7th century	Christianity reaches the Wachau via Salzburg.
9th century	In 823 the name "Wahowa" is first used for a small part of the Wachau.
10th century	Shipping flourishes on the Danube: wine, salt and wood are transported up- and downriver. The Babenbergs make Melk their royal residence.
11th–13th centuries	The Crusades herald a boom for the towns on the banks of the Danube. The robber barons also get their share. In 1192, England's Richard the Lion-Heart, on his way back from the Third Crusade, is imprisoned in the Kuenringerburg above Dürnstein. He is discovered by his minstrel and released after payment of a ransom. Part of the 13th-century *Song of the Nibelungs* is set in the Wachau. Melk is mentioned as "Medelike".
14th century	In 1338, a plague of locusts destroys the entire fruit harvest of the Wachau.
15th century	During the war against Hungary, Krems is besieged by King Matthias Corvinus, and the other towns of the Wachau also suffer.
16th century	War against the Turks. A major fire sweeps Krems in 1529, and in 1548 the town of Melk is almost totally destroyed by a blaze. It is rebuilt in the Renaissance style.
17th century	During the Thirty Years' War, Swedish troops burn Dürnstein, leave the Kuenringerburg in ruins, and besiege Krems and Stein. In 1680 the Wachau is hit by a catastrophic plague.
18th century	Jakob Prandtauer is commissioned to rebuild the abbey of Melk. After his death, his pupil Josef Munggenast completes the work. The parish church of Krems is also built at this time.
19th century	In 1829 the Danube Steamship Company *(Donau-Dampfschifffahrtsgesellschaft)* is founded. Until World War I it is the biggest inland shipping company in the world.
20th century	In 1929 the Danube freezes as far as Spitz in the Wachau.

Sightseeing

Melk

Mentioned in the *Song of the Nibelungs* as "Medelike", Melk was settled as early as the 9th century, but was not to receive a charter until 1898. In the Middle Ages, the salt, wine and iron trades flourished here. In 1548 a fire reduced the town virtually to ashes, and the buildings were rebuilt in the Renaissance style. (The baroque façades date from the 18th century.)

After a short walk around the town, follow the Stiftsweg leading up to the magnificent Benedictine abbey, Stift Melk. Having crossed the forecourt, you find yourself confronted by the impressive eastern façade of the monastery. Via the Prälatenhof (Prelates' Court) you reach a magnificent staircase which climbs to the **Kaiserzimmer** (Imperial Rooms). In the modern museum you can acquaint yourself with the secular and spiritual history of the abbey. Amongst the showpieces is the famous Cross of Melk inlaid with pearls and precious stones, and celebrated in legend. It is claimed that the cross was stolen in the 12th century. It found its way back to the monastery by mysterious means —floating against the current upstream from Vienna!

The **Marmorsaal** (Marble Hall), light, bright and richly decorated with ceiling frescoes and other ornaments, was used as a dining room and guest room in former days. Pass through the balconies to the **Bibliothek**, its magnificent inlaid shelves weighed down with some 100,000 precious books and 1888 manuscripts. Richly decorated with frescoes, the room is a work of art in its own right.

A spiral staircase leads down into the **Stiftskirche** (Abbey Church), where you can admire the high altar, the pulpit, the beautifully carved confessionals and choir stalls, the ceiling frescoes by Johann Michael Rottmayr and the great organ.

Dürnstein

This pretty little baroque town nestles on the bank of the Danube and can only be explored on foot: you have to leave your car on the edge of town.

Dürnstein is famous mainly for the **Kuenringerburg**, the castle in which Richard I of England, the Lion-Heart, was held captive in the 12th century. He had offended the Babenberg Duke Leopold V during the Third Crusade, and was recognized and captured in Vienna whilst attempting to slip away up the Danube valley. Accord-

Exquisite painting adorns the ceiling of Melk abbey's Marble Hall.

ing to the legend, his faithful minstrel Blondel traced him here to Dürnstein by singing the king's favourite songs outside every castle until he came to the right one and heard Richard join in the chorus. After the Swedish onslaught in 1645, only ruins remained of the castle. The 20-minute ascent is pleasantly rewarded with breathtaking views of the river.

The **Stiftskirche** (Monastic Church), resplendent in blue and white, has one of the finest baroque towers in the whole of Austria. Walk through the ornate portal and the quiet courtyard to reach the interior, where the three divine virtues Faith, Hope and Charity watch over the carved pulpit (and over the portal). The cloister is worth a visit.

On Hauptstrasse, bounded to the east by the Kremser Tor, you can see many pretty **town houses** from the 16th to 18th centuries, some of them with sgraffito decoration. On the same street, you will find the late-Gothic **Rathaus** (town hall) with its fine courtyard. Only ruins remain of the former **Klarissinenkloster** (Convent of the Poor Clares).

You can take part in a wine tasting in the **Kellerschlössl** (1715), with its huge old wine cellar and rich decoration of frescoes and reliefs.

Krems

The centre of the Wachau's wine industry is considered to be the most beautiful town in Lower Austria. Krems and the neighbouring town of Stein, linked by the appropriately named village of Und ("and" in German), have merged together as they have grown in size.

If you walk westwards along Untere Landstrasse, past the Kleines Sgraffitohaus, you will come to the **Simandlbrunnen** "Simon's Fountain), depicting the character in question returning home from an evening's drinking to a none-too-gentle reception from his angry wife.

Cross Wegscheid to reach **Hoher Markt**, the town's oldest square. Here stands the resplendent Gothic **Gozzo-Burg**, built in the 13th century in Italian style by the municipal judge Gozzo. In the **Piaristenkirche**, the church in Piaristengasse, there's a particularly extensive collection of paintings by Martin Johann Schmidt (1718–1801), a prolific artist familiarly known as Kremser Schmidt, who adorned most of the region's churches. The **Pfarrkirche St. Veit** (St Vitus parish church) is a fine baroque building decorated by eminent artists. The large ceiling frescoes

---

AUSTRIAN WINES

The Viennese are happy to drink white wine with either meat or fish. The best known of Austrian whites, Gumpoldskirchner, has the full body and bouquet of its southern vineyards. But the Viennese give equal favour to their own Grinzinger, Nussdorfer, Sieveringer and Neustifter. From the Danube valley, with an extra natural sparkle, come the Kremser, Dürnsteiner and Langenloiser.

To enjoy them to the full, visit a "Heuriger", a typically Austrian institution, where you drink young white wine and help yourself to a buffet of hot and cold snacks, usually including tasty cheese and cold meats, salads and crispy bread.

and the All Souls Altar, at the back of the church and to the right, are by Kremser Schmidt. The former Dominican church today houses the **Weinstadt museum** of wine-making. You will see sculptures from the medieval and baroque periods, paintings and etchings by Kremser Schmidt, and artefacts from the wine-growers' guild.

The **Stein Gate** at the end of Obere Landstrasse was part of the medieval city wall. Its round Gothic towers date from the 15th century.

Steiner Landstrasse in **Stein** boasts several fine buildings. The **Minoritenkirche** (Minorites' Church) was built during the transition from Romanesque to Gothic, and this stylistic blend gives the building its particular character. The **Pfarrhof** (presbytery), with its magnificent rococo stucco work, is also worth a visit. The mighty seven-storey tower of the Frauenbergkirche rises above the town.

Dining Out

In the Wachau you may as well cast any good intentions to the winds and indulge yourself to the full on local specialities.

Among typical main courses you will find hearty goulash (*Herrengulasch*), roast meats (*Rostbraten*) with garlic, and *Bauernschmaus*, which literally means "farmer's feast": bread dumplings, sauerkraut, meat and sausage. With the Danube on the doorstep, fish is an essential item on any menu: trout, zander (pike-perch), pike and carp are prepared in various mouth-watering ways.

Lovers of hot puddings will find plenty to satisfy their appetites: *Kaiserschmarren* (a sort of pancake with raisins), and if you can face another dumpling, *Topfen-, Marillen-* and *Germknödel* (filled with apricots, curd cheese or plums), and much more besides.

To go with your "Jause" (afternoon cup of coffee) there are plenty of mouthwatering pastries and strudel, stuffed with poppy seeds, nuts, curd cheese or apricots.

Shopping

Craft products include pottery, embroidery work and jewellery. Small watercolours or copper-plate engravings of the local landscape make a charming gift for your friends or a memento if you want to spoil yourself. Dolls in traditional Wachau costume *(Dirndl)* with golden bonnets are a popular buy, and a good bottle of local wine or apricot schnapps, Marillen-brand, will go down well.

Banks and currency exchange. Open Monday–Friday 8 or 9 a.m.–3 or 3.30 p.m., until 5.30 p.m. on Thursdays. Small branches generally close for lunch, between 12.30 and 1.30 p.m. Money can also be changed at railway stations and post offices, and you'll have no problems finding automatic cash-distributors in Vienna's city centre, notably around St Stephan's Cathedral and on Kärntner Strasse.

Climate. The Wachau's favoured climate means plenty of sunshine and mild temperatures. Spring starts here at the beginning of March! On the other hand, Vienna has a continental climate. Winters are often harsh, with occasional snow. In January and February the temperature may drop to –15 °C (–9°F). In summer it may climb to 30 °C (86 °F).

Clothing. People tend to dress elegantly for the theatre, concerts and the opera.

Credit cards. The major cards are accepted in hotels, restaurants and large shops.

Currency. The Euro, divided into 100 cents. Coins: 1, 2, 5, 10, 20 and 50 cents, 1 and 2 euros; banknotes: 5, 10, 20, 50, 100, 200 and 500 euros.

Ferries. Mostly in operation 7 a.m.–7 p.m. during the summer months. Car ferries operate at Spitz and Weissenkirchen.

Media. The principal foreign newspapers are sold in kiosks on the day of publication. Hotels usually have cable TV and the main English-language information channels such as BBC World and CNN.

Post offices. Open Monday–Friday 8 a.m.–noon and 2–6 p.m, Saturday 8–10 a.m. Not all post offices are open on Saturdays.

Safety. Do not carry large amounts of cash, and when you go sightseeing, leave your valuables and important documents in your hotel or cruise ship safe.

Shops. Most shops open Monday to Friday 9 a.m.–6 p.m. or 6.30 p.m. and Saturday 9 a.m.–6 p.m. Some have late closing at 7.30 p.m. on Thursday or Friday.

Time. GMT +1 in winter, GMT +2 from end March to end October.

Tipping. A service charge is automatically added to restaurant bills, but it is customary to round the bill up by about 10%. You should also leave a small tip in cafés.

VIENNA

City of Legends

As the old capital of the Habsburg empire—which included not only Slavs and Hungarians but also Germans, Spaniards, Italians and Belgians—Vienna has always been an outpost and gateway of Western civilization. A melting pot long before New York, the city has perpetually defied a simple national label. Its language is German—with a distinctive Viennese touch. But the city and people have too much Balkan and Latin in them to be compared with Hamburg, Berlin or Frankfurt.

The town's tree-lined Ringstrasse, encircling the Inner City, compares favourably with the airy sweep of Parisian boulevards. In every sense the heart of the city, it has baroque palaces, elegant shops, convivial cafés, the illustrious Burgtheater and Staatsoper (State Opera) and narrow medieval streets, winding around the cathedral.

Outside the Ring, the city sprawls through 22 other districts with plentiful parks and even farms and vineyards inside the city limits. Vienna has space to relax, a city in a rural setting that makes the attitude to life of its 1.5 million population more easygoing than in most modern cities.

This pleasant atmosphere always comes as a surprise to visitors. Most of the people still seem to have time for the courtesies of the old days. Shopkeepers like to call their regular customers by aristocratic titles that, constitutionally, should have disappeared after World War I, or at least by a nicely inflated professional title.

No word better describes the ideal of Viennese life than *Gemütlichkeit*. Literally untranslatable, *gemütlich* means agreeable, comfortable. As unmistakable as a Viennese smile, it is the quality that takes the rough edges off life.

A BRIEF HISTORY

1st–3rd centuries	Romans set up a garrison—Vindobona—on the Danube and drive off successive invasions by Teutons, Slavs and other tribes. Emperor Marcus Aurelius leads fighting against the barbarians and dies in Vindobona in 180.
4th–12th centuries	Christianity is introduced; barbarian invasions continue. The Babenberg dynasty drives out the Magyars around 1000, and they are named hereditary Dukes of Austria by the Holy Roman Emperor in 1156.

A BRIEF HISTORY

13th century	Vienna's first "golden age" begins. Art, trade, and handicrafts thrive; Scottish and Irish monks establish a monastery; churches, residences and new thoroughfares are built. The last of the Babenbergs dies in 1246; Ottokar II of Bohemia succeeds to the regency. He is supplanted by Rudolf von Habsburg in 1278.
14th–16th centuries	Rudolf der Stifter (the Founder) creates the university in 1365. In 1469 Vienna is granted Rome's approval as a bishopric. Hungarian King Matthias Corvinus occupies the city from 1485 to 1490. In 1529 Turks under Suleiman the Magnificent lay siege. The Innere Stadt holds firm and Suleiman retreats. The Reformation reaches Vienna but Catholicism remains predominant.
17th century	Emperor Leopold I ushers Vienna into its glorious baroque era. The construction of magnificent palaces and churches begins. The plague strikes in 1679; the Turks lay a second unsuccessful siege in 1683.
18th century	Emperor Charles VI is succeeded by his daughter Maria Theresa. Her relatively benevolent 40-year reign extends its influence to the capital's citizens and Vienna blooms as a musical city.
19th century	Napoleon's armies arrive in 1805. Emperor Franz I gives his daughter Marie-Louise in diplomatic marriage to Napoleon in 1810. The Congress of Vienna completes its territorial discussions in June 1815 and provides Europe with a framework for international diplomacy which is to last a hundred years. The Ringstrasse complex of aristocratic residences is developed and the new opera built.
20th century–present	The Habsburg empire ends with World War I, which leaves Vienna in economic and social ruin. Chancellor Dollfuss is murdered by Austrian Nazis in 1934. Hitler annexes Austria and it becomes a province of "Greater Germany" from 1938 to 1945. After the war Vienna is divided into four sectors under the joint four-power administration of the Americans, Russians, British and French. In 1955 Austria is given independent neutral status and enters a prosperous new period of economic recovery. It joins the EU in 1995.

Sightseeing

The best way to appreciate the city centre is on foot, but for a more romantic introduction to the town, try a **Fiaker tour**. The two-horse open carriages have been in business since the 17th century, and their elegantly turned out drivers have a fund of amusing stories to put you in the right mood.

The cathedral, **Stephansdom**, will draw you like a magnet; it is the ideal starting point for your visit. With its Romanesque western façade, Gothic tower and baroque altars, the cathedral is a marvellous example of the Viennese genius for harmonious compromise, melding the austerity, dignity and exuberance of those great architectural styles. The Romanesque origins are visible in the Heidentürme and statuary depicting, among others, a griffin and Samson fighting a lion. The transformation into the Gothic structure we see today was carried out mainly during the 14th and 15th centuries.

From the north tower you have a fine view of the city, and of the huge Pummerin bell cast from melted-down Turkish cannons after the 1683 siege was repelled. The present bell is a recast version of the original destroyed during World War II.

Inside the church, look in the centre aisle for the charming carved Gothic **pulpit** by Anton Pilgram. At the head of the spiral staircase, the sculptor has placed Augustine, Gregory, Jerome and Ambrose, fathers of the Church. He also defied the customary medieval anonymity with a sculpture of himself looking through a window under the staircase.

On the left side of the high altar you'll find the carved wooden **Wiener Neustädter Altar**; on the right side is the impressive marble **tomb** of Emperor Friedrich III, honoured by the Viennese as the man who had the city made a bishopric.

After a long visit to the Stephansdom (and a coffee in one of the pleasant *Kaffeehäuser* in the area) head for the **Mozarthaus Vienna** just southeast of the cathedral. Here, from 1784 to 1787, lived Wolfgang Amadeus Mozart. The building was renovated to re-open on January 27, 2006 for the 250th anniversary of Mozart's birth. He wrote 11 of his piano concertos here, as well as the *Marriage of Figaro* and many other pieces. He died a pauper in the musty Rauhensteingasse not far away; here he completed *The Magic Flute* and was working on the *Requiem* at the time of his death. His coffin was blessed in an anonymous ceremony for that day's dead.

Stroll back to the **Kärntner Strasse**, the city's main north-south thoroughfare where many of Vienna's smartest shops can be found. Today it is a traffic-free pedestrian zone with open-air cafés down the middle of the street. At the Stephansdom end of Kärntner Strasse pass through the Stock-im-Eisen square to the **Graben**, also a pedestrian zone. The **Pestsäule** (Pillar of the Plague) is a somewhat grotesque monument commemorating the town's deliverance from the plague in 1679.

The **Peterskirche** (St Peter's Church), just off the Graben, provides a splendid example of how Viennese baroque manages more often than not to be both sumptuous and intimate. Designed by Johann Lukas, it has an unusual oval-shaped nave. The curved pews are all decorated with three sculpted angels.

From here you can make a short detour through the old Jewish quarter to the **Ruprechtskirche**, easily recognizable by its ivy-covered façade.

Return to the **Hoher Markt**, which was the forum of the Roman settlement, Vindobona. A small museum displays the remains of two Roman houses laid bare by a 1945 bombardment.

To the west, follow Salvatorgasse, pausing to admire the superb Renaissance porch of the **Salvatorkapelle**, a happy marriage of Italian design and Austrian late-Gothic sculpture. Beyond it is a slender jewel of 14th-century Gothic, the church of **Maria am Gestade** ("Mary on the Banks"—of the River Danube that used to flow directly beneath it).

Walk back across the Judenplatz to the spacious **Am Hof**, the largest square of the old city. An elaborate baroque building makes a grand fire station. From here make for the **Freyung** triangle flanked by the **Schottenkirche** (Scots' Church), founded by Scottish and Irish Benedictine monks in the 12th century.

Ring

Before tackling the Hofburg, it's a good idea to go around the Ring, probably the greatest single urban achievement of Franz Joseph. This boulevard encircling the Innere Stadt was mapped out in the 1860s along the ramparts Joseph II had begun clearing 80 years before.

Start your walk at the west end of the Schottenring, in front of the **Votivkirche**, a neo-Gothic church built after Franz Joseph survived an assassination attempt in 1853. Next to it

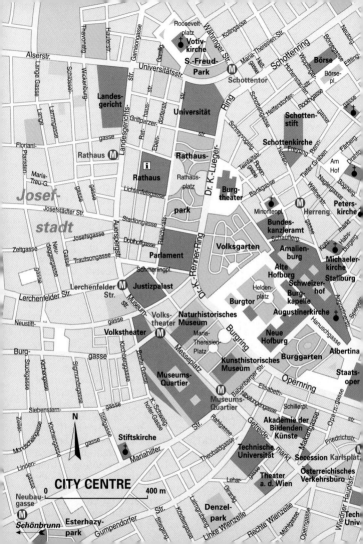

are the university and **Rathaus** (Town Hall) with a pleasant park, but proceed along the Innere Stadt side, past the impressive **Burgtheater**, a high temple of the German stage. Beyond it is the lovely **Volksgarten**. Its cafés and open-air concerts carry on a tradition that began with the café music of the Strauss family.

The **Burggarten**, the park of Hofburg, leads to the **Staatsoper** (State Opera). It's worth taking a guided tour here before attending a performance.

On Karlsplatz, not far from the opera house, stands the huge **Karlskirche**, undoubtedly the most important of the city's baroque churches. Its visual impact has diminished since the building of the Ringstrasse. However, the cool, sober interior remains unchanged, with a subdued marble decor and an oval ground-plan similar to that of the Peterskirche. In front of the

church, a massive Henry Moore sculpture in a reflector pool provides a striking contrast. Also on the Karlsplatz is Otto Wagner's fanciful **Stadtbahnpavillon** (an old underground station) with its graceful green, gold and white Jugendstil motif of sunflowers and tulips. Close by you will notice a house with a golden cupola, built in 1898 by architect Joseph Maria Olbrich. In the basement is a frieze by Gustav Klimt, inspired by Beethoven.

The Hofburg

Though the Habsburgs are long gone, Vienna remains an imperial city—an aura enhanced by its palaces.

The most imposing is the Hofburg, home of Austria's rulers since the 13th century. Start your visit right in the middle at the

Schweizerhof, named after the Swiss Guard that used to be housed there. Here Ottokar of Bohemia built a fortress in 1275–76 to defend himself against Rudolf von Habsburg. He wasn't successful and the Habsburgs moved in; they strengthened the fortifications because of the unruly Viennese outside.

The **Burgkapelle** (Castle Chapel), tucked away in the northern corner of the Schweizerhof, was built in 1449. Originally Gothic, it was redone in baroque style and then partially restored to its original form in 1802. The Vienna Boys' Choir (Wiener Sängerknaben) sings Mass here every Sunday morning, except in July and August.

Between 1558 and 1565 Ferdinand I built the **Stallburg** (outside the main Hofburg complex on the northeast side of Reitschulgasse) as a home for his son Archduke Maximilian.

Still in Renaissance style is Rudolf II's **Amalienburg**, built between 1575 and 1611 by Italian architect Pietro Ferrabosco.

Leopold I launched the city's baroque era with his **Leopoldinischer Trakt** (Leopold Wing), which now serves as the home of the Austrian presidency.

Karl VI continued the Habsburg's self-confident traditions with the **Reichskanzlei** (Imperial Chancellery), where Franz Joseph was later to have his apartments, the Hofbibliothek (library) and the Winterreitschule (the winter quarters of the Spanish Riding School).

Josefsplatz is a marvellously harmonious baroque square, with an equestrian statue of Joseph II in the middle. Inside the old library, the oval **Prunksaal** (Great Hall), with frescoes and walnut bookshelves, is one of the most beautiful baroque interiors in the world.

Just off the Josefsplatz is the **Augustinerkirche**, the church that the Habsburgs favoured for their great events. The façade of this Gothic and baroque structure matches the library and Redoutensaal. The church they chose to be buried in, the Kapuzinerkirche, lies outside the Hofburg. Its **Kaisergruft** (Imperial Vault) contains some 140 assorted Habsburgs—emperors, empresses, archdukes and other members of the royal family.

The **Spanische Reitschule** (Spanish Riding School) must not be missed, even if it is just to see the splendid arcades supported by 46 columns. The white Lippizaner horses are trained to walk and dance with a delicacy that many ballet-dancers might envy. Tickets for performances must be booked at least six months in advance; a 83 more convenient option is to watch the horses train.

For an idea of the human scale of what turned into the Habsburgs' folly, you should take the guided tour of the **Imperial Apartments** *(Kaiserappartements)*, entrance on Michaelerplatz. Some of the rooms now comprise the **Sissi Museum**.

When you leave the Hofburg, take the Schauflergasse to **Ballhausplatz** to see the elegant 18th-century residence of the Austrian chancellors. One of them, Dollfuss, was assassinated here in July 1934.

Schönbrunn

If the Hofburg is the oversized expression of a dynasty that outgrew its own virility, Schönbrunn is the smiling, serene expression of the personality of

---

SISSI: MYTH AND REALITY

In the 1950s, the cinema drew a picture of Sissi that was kitschy and divorced from all reality. Empress Elisabeth (1837–98) was an intelligent and cultivated woman who worried little about court etiquette and much about the destiny of the Hungarian people. She spent a long time in the vicinity of Budapest. The sensitive empress was very much concerned about her physical appearance. For this she imposed iron discipline with exercise and a constant diet. From her 30th birthday, she refused to let herself be photographed.

After her marriage with her cousin Franz Joseph at the age of 16, she had to exchange a hitherto fairly free life in Bavaria for the strict supervision of her mother-in-law, Sophie, who also later took over the education of the children. The empress fell ill and took refuge in the milder climate of Madeira—the first of a long series of journeys abroad.

In June 1867, her efforts for more recognition for the Hungarian people reaped their reward. The imperial couple were crowned King and Queen of Hungary: the dual monarchy was born. Even this, however, did not keep Sissi in the palace. After she had given her husband four children, she decided at 40 to distance herself still further from court and pursue her passion for poetry and travel.

The empress suffered a terrible blow when her son, Rudolf committed suicide. In 1889, in mysterious circumstances, the heir to the throne took his life, along with that of his mistress, Baroness Mary Vetsera, on the royal estate of Mayerling. Nine years later, when out walking on the Quai du Mont-Blanc in Geneva, Elisabeth was stabbed to death by the Italian anarchist Luigi Lucheni.

one woman—Maria Theresa, Archduchess of Austria, Queen of Bohemia and Hungary.

To appreciate the emphasis Schönbrunn puts on pleasure, rather than imperial pomp, it's best to visit the **gardens** first. The park, laid out in the classical French manner, is dominated by the **Gloriette**, a neoclassical colonnade perched on the crest of a hill. It commemorates the Austrian victory of 1757 over Frederick II's Prussian army. Today it houses a café.

East of the Neptune Fountain are the bizarre **Roman ruins**, actually built in 1778—a half-buried "Roman palace" with bits of Corinthian columns, friezes and archways.

After visiting the gardens head for the **palace**, where a guided grand tour (audioguides also available) will give you a glimpse of the sumptuous comfort in which Maria Theresa and her successors handled the affairs of state. A short tour takes in only the appartments of Franz-Josef and Sissi in the right wing. On the long tour you'll see Maria Theresa's breakfast room, decorated with the needlework of the empress and her myriad daughters; the **Spiegelsaal** (Hall of Mirrors) in which the young Mozart gave his first royal recital; the **Chinesisches Rundkabinett** (Chinese Round Room), adorned with lacquered Oriental panels, and also known as Maria Theresa's Konspirationstafelstube (roughly translatable as "dining room for plotting").

You should not miss what is known as the **Napoleon Room** (though it was once Maria Theresa's bedroom), where the emperor stayed on his way to the Battle of Austerlitz and where his son, the Duke of Reichstadt, spent his last sad years.

In the adjoining **Wagenburg** museum, you can marvel at a collection of coaches used by the imperial court.

Belvedere

Of all the palaces built by the princes, dukes and barons serving the Habsburgs, the most splendid must certainly be the Belvedere of Prince Eugene of Savoy. It is regarded as Vienna's finest flowering of baroque residential architecture.

Today the **Unteres Belvedere** and its **Orangerie** house the admirable collections of Austrian medieval and baroque art in the Barockmuseum. On the other side of the park, in the **Oberes** (or Upper) **Belvedere**, the prince held his banquets and other festivities. Nowhere will you see a finer view of the city skyline than from its **terrace**, which has changed little since Bernardo Bellotto (Canaletto the Younger) painted it in 1760.

The Other Vienna

Beyond the Innere Stadt and outside the Habsburg world of the Hofburg and Schönbrunn, there is another Vienna, the people's Vienna.

Cross the Danube Canal over the Aspernbrücke, at the junction of Franz-Josefs-Kai and Stubenring. This takes you to the **Prater** park, Vienna's own non-stop carnival (also accessible by tram or underground). If the Stephansdom had not already become the undisputed symbol of the city, the Prater's

Riesenrad (giant Ferris wheel) built in 1897 would certainly have laid a claim. Immortalized by Carol Reed's film *The Third Man* (1949), the Riesenrad, with its 14 bright red cabins taking you up for a constantly changing perspective of the city's skyline, is only part of the fair that includes roller-coasters, discotheques, shooting ranges, restaurants and beer halls.

The **Donaupark** linking the old and new Danube is more tranquil than the Prater, laid out with beautiful flower beds, and artificial lake, sports arenas and a chair-lift from which to survey it all. It also features a 250-m (827-ft) tower, the **Donauturm**, with two revolving restaurants and a public terrace featuring a view across the city south to the hills of the Wienerwald and northwest to the Abbey of Klosterneuburg.

Döbling is the most gracious of Vienna's neighbourhoods. Stretching from the Danube Canal back to the undulating slopes of the Wienerwald, Döbling includes Sievering, Grinzing, Heiligenstadt, Nussdorf and Kahlenberg. It has elegant villas, parks, vineyards and, of course, the ever popular Heurigen wine gardens.

A short detour to the north takes in the imposing Augustine abbey of **Klosterneuburg**, founded in the 12th century. The baroque palace-church is impressive but the trip is made worthwhile by the magnificent **Verdun Altar** of 1181, containing 45 enamelled panels depicting scenes from the scriptures.

Museums

Vienna's National Gallery, the **Kunsthistorisches Museum**, is outstanding. The magnificent art collection contains masterpieces by all of the European great masters—Dutch, Flemish,

FRIEDENSREICH HUNDERTWASSER (1928–2000)

Born in 1928 and christened Friedrich Stowasser, he altered his name to Friedensreich Hundertwasser (Rich in Peace Hundredwater) in 1949, after three months of study at Vienna's Academy of Fine Arts—his only formal artistic training.

Taking his inspiration from nature, the changing patterns reflected in water, the rhythms of Arabic music, he favoured the use of vibrant, saturated primary colours, and was particularly fascinated by the spiral, albeit an irregular, meandering spiral. His aversion for regular, planned architecture with strict, straight lines led him to design buildings topped with trees and houses with grass roofs where animals can graze, uneven floors and curving walls.

Hundertwasser, 460 Hommage au Tachisme (1961)

German and English to the left and Italian, Spanish and French to the right. On the ground floor are the Egyptian, Oriental, Greek and Roman art treasures and sculptures. The **Naturhistorische Museum**, has zoological, anthropological, paleontological displays and a beautiful collection of gemstones.

Nearby, the modern **MuseumsQuartier** was inaugurated in 2001. It is one of the 10 biggest cultural complexes in the world, with several museums, theatres and exhibition halls.

Austrian art is displayed in three different galleries of the **Belvedere**: the museum of medieval art, the baroque museum, and the gallery of 19th and 20th century art, with works by Klimt, Schiele, Kokoschka, Munch and others.

The **Liechtenstein Museum** (1, Fürstengasse), is a handsome baroque palace displaying splendid art collections from early Renaissance to Romanticism.

Most of the Habsburg fortune can be seen in the Hofburg. The **Schatzkammer** (Treasury), in the Schweizerhof, contains a dazzling display of the insignia of the old Holy Roman Empire. These include the Imperial Crown of pure unalloyed gold, set with pearls and unpolished emeralds, sapphires and rubies. The **Silberkammer** (Imperial Silver Collection) exhibits the priceless Chinese, Japanese, French Sèvres and German Meissen porcelain services amassed by the Habsburgs over six centuries as well as sumptuous silverware.

The **Albertina** is home to the world's greatest graphic art collection, shown in changing exhibitions. It includes thousands of drawings, watercolours and prints by Da Vinci, Dürer, Rubens, Raphael, Michelangelo, Rembrandt, but also 20th-century artists such as Klimt Schiele and Rauschenberg.

GUSTAV KLIMT

Klimt (1862–1918) was a pioneer of modern painting in Vienna. In 1897 he became the first president of the Secession group, which gathered several young artists in search of new means of expression. Having assimilated the innovative ideas and spirit of the Impressionists, Symbolists and Pre-Raphaelites, as well as the precepts of Art Nouveau, he developed a powerful personal style, at once opulent and disquieting. Among his major works, *The Kiss* is displayed at the Belvedere, while his 34-m-long Beethoven frieze can be seen in the basement of the Secession pavilion.

You can visit the Schubert, Haydn or Beethoven museums, but the best arranged of these "personal" museums, making up for the hostility with which most Viennese received him during his lifetime, is the one devoted to **Sigmund Freud**. The house that he lived in at Berggasse 19 before he had to flee the Nazis has become a mecca for students—and patients—of psychoanalysis from all over the world.

The Vienna-born painter and architect Friedensreich Hundertwasser designed the **KunstHausWien**, on Untere Weissgerberstr. 13 in the 3rd district, using recycled material and brightly coloured ceramics. In contrast to the severity and austerity of Vienna's architecture, there are no straight lines anywhere, and everything seems slightly skewed. Despite its confusing style—or because of it—this small, private gallery is worth a visit.

The **Hundertwasser-Haus**, an apartment block on Löwengasse in the 3rd district, is another example of non-conformism and environmental

A QUICK COFFEE?

Not likely. In Vienna a coffee is to be savoured slowly, not swallowed down in one gulp. The choice is confusingly large. Here are a few explanations:
Brauner: black with a dash of milk.
Einspänner: black with whipped cream, served in a tall glass.
Eiskaffee: black with whipped cream and vanilla ice cream.
Kapuziner: cappuccino, topped
with a dollop of whipped cream and sprinkled with powdered chocolate.
Melange: frothy and milky, maybe with a blob of whipped cream.
Mocca: strong and black, most often espresso.
Türkischer: boiling hot and sweet.

awareness. For the façade, recycled bricks and other materials were used. No two windows are alike. A 5-km (3-mile) ceramic strip circles the façade and two onion-shaped cupolas adorn the roof.

Dining Out

The emperors, archdukes and generals have gone; not so the Bohemian dumplings, Hungarian goulash, Polish stuffed cabbage and Serbian shashlik. But there are Austrian specialities too: *Wienerschnitzel*, a large thinly sliced cutlet of veal sauteed in a coating of egg and seasoned breadcrumbs; *Backhendl*, boned deep-fried chicken prepared like *Wienerschnitzel; Tafelspitz*, boiled beef, a Viennese favourite; or *Knödel*, dumplings served with soups and with the meat dish, studded with pieces of liver or bacon.

Dumplings are also served as a dessert with hot apricot inside (*Marillenknödel*) or with cream cheese (*Topfenknödel*). As for pastries, the word is inseparable from Vienna itself, like "waltz", "woods", and "Danube". The variations of cherries, strawberries, hazelnuts, walnuts, apple and chocolate in tarts, pies, cakes and strudels are endless, and they are all even better topped with whipped cream

(*mit Schlag*). And join in the never-ending controversy over the most famous chocolate cake in the world, the *Sachertorte*—whether it should be split and sandwiched together with apricot jam, or just left plain.

Shopping

Not surprisingly, the most important shopping attraction in Vienna—a town preoccupied by its history—is antiques. Furniture and objets d'art from all over the old empire have somehow ended up here in the little shops in the Innere Stadt.

Still in the realm of the past are the great speciality shops for coin and stamp-collectors (where else could you expect to find mint-condition Bosnia-Herzegovina issues of 1914?).

The national Augarten porcelain workshops still turn out hand-decorated rococo chinaware. Exquisite petitpoint embroidery is available in the form of handbags, cushions and other items with flower, folk and opera motifs. You will find the more elegant shops on the Kärntnerstrasse, Graben and Kohlmarkt.

If your taste runs from the exquisite to kitsch, try your luck in the Saturday morning flea market on the Naschmarkt, with plenty of food stalls, too.

BRATISLAVA

Proud Fortress

Unlike other European capitals, the mention of Bratislava may not send people into raptures. But upon closer examination, the city reveals plenty of cultural and historical interest.

The German Pressburg, Hungarian Pozsony and Slovakian Bratislava are in fact one and the same place, its successive names testifying to a rich and varied past. Many influences have contributed to the culture of the Slovak capital, the most important being the Magyar. Bratislava was the Hungarian capital for 250 years and many Austro-Hungarian monarchs were crowned here. The Czech influence is also felt, as until 1 January 1993, the Czech and Slovak republics formed one state, in which Bratislava was subordinate to Prague.

Bratislava's geographical location has always played a part in the vicissitudes of its history.

About 60 km (37 miles) from Vienna and 200 km (124 miles) from Budapest, the city lies on the banks of the Danube, where Slovakia meets Austria and Hungary, at the foot of the Little Carpathians.

To this day, Bratislava, with 450,000 inhabitants, is one of the Danube's major ports. It has developed into an important industrial centre and venue for trade fairs. The cultural and economic focus of Slovakia, Bratislava boasts such great institutions as the Slovak Academy of the Sciences, founded in 1465 by the Hungarian King Matthias Corvinus, a conservatory and a theatre academy.

With Renaissance, baroque and rococo buildings, the Old Quarter holds a great deal of charm for visitors; those with a passion for culture and the arts will find a wealth of theatres and museums. Jazz and classical music festivals attract music lovers from all over the world.

A BRIEF HISTORY

3rd century BC–2nd century AD	The area occupied by modern Slovakia is settled by Celts, who are driven out by Germanic tribes in the 1st century BC. Towards the end of the 2nd century AD, these in their turn are ousted by the Romans under Marcus Aurelius. (The Hungarian name Pozsony is derived from the Roman Posonium.)
6th century	In the wake of Germanic tribes and Huns, Slavs settle in the Danube basin.

A BRIEF HISTORY

9th century	The Great Moravian Duke Bratislav (after whom Bratislava is named) builds a castle above the Danube.
10th–12th centuries	In 907 the town is mentioned as "Brezalauspure" (later Pressburg). After the demise of the Great Moravian Empire under the onslaught of the Magyars, Slovakia falls to Hungary. German immigrants influence the development of towns and mining.
13th century	In 1291 King Andrew III of Hungary grants Pressburg (German at that time) the rights of a free royal city.
15th century	In 1465 a Hungarian university is founded. In the Treaty of Pressburg (1491) with King Vladislav II of Bohemia, the Habsburg Holy Roman Emperor Maximilian I establishes his family's succession to the thrones of Hungary and Bohemia.
16th century	The city flourishes. After the Turks' invasion of Hungary, Bratislava becomes the capital of Habsburg Hungary in 1541 and remains so for some 250 years; the monarchs are crowned in St Martin's Cathedral.
18th century	The city enjoys a renaissance under the rule of Maria Theresa: magnificent baroque palaces are built. However, in 1783 Joseph II transfers the capital back to Buda, and Bratislava's importance declines.
19th century	After the Battle of Austerlitz, Napoleon and Franz I of Austria sign the Peace of Pressburg (1805). From 1825–48 the Hungarian parliament is held in the city. The Slovaks make their national and social demands heard, but Slovakia still remains subject to Hungary.
20th century– present	Czechoslovakia comes into being in 1918. From 1939–45 Slovakia is independent, but maintains close ties with the German Reich. In April 1945 Soviet troops capture Bratislava, and in May Slovakia is handed back to the Prague government. After the peaceful separation of the Czech and Slovak Republics, Bratislava becomes capital of Slovakia on the first of January 1993. Far-reaching privatization of state concerns takes place. Since its separation from the Czech Republic, Slovakia has been forging stronger economic links with the West. It joins the EU in 2004.

Sightseeing

Castle *(Hrad)*

Visible from afar, this majestic building with its four corner towers stands prominently on a hill above the Danube. The fortress was built in the Middle Ages, but alterations took place in the 17th and 18th centuries. It was destroyed by fire in 1811 and rebuilt only after 1953. Those rooms accessible to the public hold part of the collections of the Slovakian National Museum, the Treasury and an exhibition which illustrates the history of the castle and of Slovakia. (The remaining rooms are used as government offices.)

The **Castle Gardens**, created in the reign of Maria Theresa, offer a breathtaking view of the Old Quarter and the Danube.

Old Quarter

Leave the gardens by the Gothic Corvinus Gate, and descend the Castle Steps *(Zámocké schody)* to the Old Quarter. In its narrow streets, ideal for exploring on foot, you'll discover Gothic, Renaissance and baroque palaces, churches and historical monuments round almost every corner.

The Castle Steps open onto Beblavého Street, which boasts the finest rococo building in the city: the **House of the Good Shepherd** *(Dom u dobrého pastiera)*. Here you'll find an interesting clock museum.

Diagonally opposite on the expressway (use the subway!), you'll see the 14th-century **St Martin's Cathedral** *(Dóm sv. Martina)*. With its three naves, it is one of the most beautiful examples of Gothic architecture in the whole of Slovakia. Between the years 1563 and 1830, 19 Austro-Hungarian monarchs were crowned here, a fact commemorated by the golden crown which tops the cathedral spire. The generously proportioned interior has been altered many times in the course of the centuries. The impressive bronze of St Martin, the city's patron saint, is the work of the famous Viennese sculptor Donner.

From the cathedral, take the pretty route along Panská Street, lined with neat Renaissance and baroque palaces, to the Main Square. During the restoration of the **Pálffy Palace** *(Pálfyho palác)*, archaeological remains from Great Moravian and even Celtic times were discovered. These finds are displayed here alongside works of art from the City Gallery.

The palaces around **Main Square** *(Hlavné námestie)* bear witness to its former greatness. Of particular interest is the **Old Town Hall** *(Stará radnica)* on

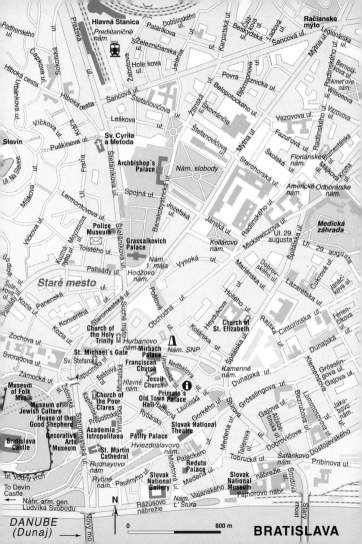

the eastern side of the square, the city's oldest secular building (1325). Public functions take place in the courtyard here during the yearly summer festival. The building also houses the collections of the **City Museum** *(Mestské múzeum),* which will better acquaint you with the history of Bratislava from its origins to the present day. Take a look also at the Renaissance Roland's Fountain (1572) in front of the Town Hall.

If you head in a northeasterly direction, you will come shortly to the **Primate's Palace** *(Primaciálny palác)* on the square of the same name. This powerful neoclassical building was constructed at the end of the 18th century. In its Mirror Hall, Napoleon and Emperor Franz I of Austria signed the Treaty of Pressburg after the Battle of Austerlitz. Part of the art collection of the City Gallery can be found here.

Just a few steps further on stands the house in which the composer Johann Nepomuk Hummel was born. Today it is a **museum** with documents and artefacts from his life.

Return now to Franciscan Square *(Františkánske námestie),* which adjoins Main Square to the north. The principal points of interest here are the baroque 17th-century **Jesuit**

Church *(Kostol jezuitov)* and the Gothic **Franciscan Church** *(Kostol františkánov),* the oldest building in the town centre. It has been altered many times, and was given a baroque façade in the 18th century. The Gothic Chapel of St John was left untouched.

Opposite stands the magnificent rococo **Mirbach Palace** *(Mirbachov palác).* The inner courtyard with its 19th-century fountain makes an attractive venue for concerts. Within the palace there's a gallery of paintings, together with six marvellous 17th-century tapestries.

Heading in a westerly direction, you come to **St Michael's Gate** *(Michalská brána),* part of the former fortifications of the city. The tower, now 51 m (167 ft) high, has grown since it was first built at the beginning of the 14th century, as extrastoreys were added over the years. In 1758 the tower was crowned with a baroque cupola, upon which St Michael sits enthroned. From the top, you have a fine view of the old town.

On the corner of Huranovo and Októbrové squares are the baroque **Church of the Holy Trinity** *(Kostol trinitárov)* and its monastery (1715–25).

A flight of steps leads to the picturesque old Klariská Street and the **Church of the Poor**

Clares *(Kostol Klarisiek),* with a late-Gothic belltower that provides a conspicuous landmark in the old town. This church, too, has been altered many times, and today it is the venue for concerts and functions.

Crossing narrow Bastová St, you arrive at Michalská and then Ventúrska streets, which lead down to the Danube. In former times, these streets were mainly used as a thoroughfare by merchants, but now they are lined with shops, bars and restaurants—alongside historical buildings such as the baroque University Library, which until 1848 was the home of the Hungarian parliament. The building that once housed the **Academia Istropolitana**—the first Hungarian (or Slovak) university, founded in 1465—is now occupied by the Music Academy.

Major theatres, museums and hotels are grouped in the elegant district between the Danube *(Dunaj)* and the greenery of wide Hviezdoslavovo Square. At its eastern end stands the **Slovak National Theatre** *(Slovenské národné divadlo),* built in 1886 in neo-Renaissance style. Operas and concerts are performed nearby in the **Reduta**

Palace, the home of the Slovak Philharmonic Orchestra.

Directly on the bank of the Danube, you'll find the **Slovak National Gallery** *(Slovenská národná galéria)* with older and contemporary art, and the **Slovak National Museum** *(Slovenská národné múzeum)* displaying botanical, mineralogical and other exhibits.

The modern cable-stayed **Danube bridge** *(Novy Most)* is surmounted by a single 86-m (282-ft) column, at the top of which is perched a panoramic restaurant, providing a view of both old and new towns.

Overlooking the river, the **Danubiana Art Gallery**, 15 km (24 miles) south of town, looks like a Roman galley about to sail forth. It opened in 2000.

Dining Out

Generally speaking, dishes are good and inexpensive, nourishing and often strongly spiced. As well as the restaurant *(restaurace),* there's the wine cellar *(vinárna)* and—for lovers of coffee and the sweet things in life—the café and cake shop *(cukrárna).*

Try the following specialities: spicy beef goulash à la Bratislava or fiery shish kebabs with pork, beef and lamb (together with ham, sausage, peppers and onions). Side dishes include potato concoctions like dumplings. Smoked cheese is another speciality, fried with ham and served with tartare sauce.

To drink, try beer *(pivo)* or wine *(víno)*. Local wines are mostly from the Veltliner, Sylvaner and Riesling grape varieties, and have sonorous names such as *Malokarpatské zlato* ("Gold from the Little Carpathians"). Then there are all sorts of spirits, like *borovicka* (gin-like), *slivovica* (plum brandy) or *marhulovica* (apricot brandy).

Shopping

Gifts include embroidery and lace, handpainted pottery and porcelain, jewellery, wood carvings and other craft objects. There is a wide variety of fine crystal glass. Have a good look around in the pretty shops and boutiques of the Old Quarter to find craft products and all kinds of souvenirs.

PRACTICAL INFORMATION

Banks. Generally open Monday–Friday 8 a.m.–5 p.m. Money can also be changed in bureaux de change, larger hotels, many shops and in post offices.

Credit cards, travellers cheques. Internationally recognized credit cards are accepted in larger hotels, restaurants and shops. Travellers cheques (best in euros or US dollars) can be changed in banks and exchange bureaus.

Currency. The currency is the Slovak crown (*Slovenská koruna,* abbreviated Sk). One crown = 100 heller (*halér,* plural *halierov*). Coins: 50 heller to 10 crowns. Notes: 20 to 5000 crowns.

Language. The official language is Slovakian. Czech, Hungarian, English and German are also spoken.

Post offices. Monday–Friday 8 a.m.–6 p.m, Saturday 8 a.m.–noon.

Shops. Usually open Monday–Friday 9 a.m.–6 or 7 p.m. and Saturday 9 a.m.–noon or 1 p.m. Some shops also open on Sunday mornings. Smaller shops close for lunch noon–2 p.m.

Transport. Buses and trams mostly operate 4.30 a.m.–midnight. Taxis are cheap.

BUDAPEST

Paris of the East

The city of Budapest conjures up a string of flattering adjectives: dramatic, enchanting, glamorous, magical. It's difficult to decide from which angle the "Paris of the East" is most breathtaking: looking over the majestic river towards the monumental expanse of Pest from the heights of Buda, or rather in the direction of the hills and towers of Buda from Pest down below.

The mighty Danube, second-longest river in Europe, flows through the heart of Hungary's capital, and is as essential to its fascination as the Thames is to London or the Seine to Paris. Long, elegant boulevards and stately buildings enhance the Parisian atmosphere, as do the romantic riverside walkways and the general air of pleasure in the good things in life. One of those good things is a soak in a thermal bath, for Budapest is a highly reputed health resort.

Buda, the old town of Obuda, and Pest were separate entities until 1849, when the first permanent bridge was built over the Danube. They did not legally become one until 1873, and even now the city's component parts fit together like pieces of a mismatched jigsaw puzzle. Buda's hills, reaching almost to the river, represent the last ripples of the Transdanubian mountains, while Pest stands on the very edge of the awesomely flat Great Plain.

Politics and geography contrived to make Budapest the main point of contact between Eastern and Western Europe, and popular with tourists from both sides of the postwar ideological divide. The city was the show window for a "goulash communism" that made Hungary the envy of Soviet bloc consumers. The red stars have now disappeared and those days are forgotten; Budapest is now resolutely Western-looking and seems to be on *everyone's* travel agenda.

Budapest was devastated by World War II, and some of its buildings still bear the scars of conflict. But thanks to inspired restoration, the city has recovered most of its former glory. With its venerable buildings, splendid panoramas, quaint medieval streets and museums of every kind, it's an exciting place to visit. When you feel tired, pause for a relaxing wallow in one of the city's many Turkish baths. At night, what could be more romantic than dining to the sound of gypsy violins as you watch the lights play on the Danube—without question Budapest's trump card.

A BRIEF HISTORY

3rd century BC–14th century AD	Celts build a stronghold on Buda's Gellért Hill dominating the Danube. The region is on the Roman Empire's main line of defence against the barbarians. When Rome weakens, Attila the Hun reigns here until his death in 453. Magyar tribes migrate across the Carpathian mountains to the central Hungarian plain in 896. The first king, Stephen I, oversees the conversion of his people to Christianity. After a Mongol invasion in the 13th century, King Béla IV revives the nation, building a number of fortified towns. The Árpád dynasty dies out in 1301, and foreign kings rule.
15th–18th centuries	A Turkish invasion is repelled in 1456. The victor's son, Matthias Corvinus, rules during Hungary's Golden Age (1458–1490). The Turks return in 1526, and this time they stay for 150 years. When they are finally routed in 1686, Hungary becomes part of the Austrian Empire. An unsuccessful war for independence rages from 1703 to 1711. Despite political dissatisfaction, the country makes great economic strides under the Austrian regime.
19th century	Another revolt, in 1848–49, is crushed by the combined forces of Austria and Russia. In 1867 the Dual Monarchy is established. The cities of Pest, Buda and Obuda merge in 1873 to form Budapest, the capital.
20th century–present	As part of the Austro-Hungarian Empire, Hungary supports Germany during World War I, with disastrous results. World War II is equally catastrophic: the country is occupied by Hitler's troops in 1944, and when Budapest finally falls to the Soviets a year later, only one in four of the city's buildings is still intact. Hungary becomes a Soviet satellite, and undergoes sweeping nationalization. The uprising of 1956 leads to a new administration, under János Kádár, aimed at improving economic conditions and relaxing political severities. In 1989's whirlwind of ideological changes, Hungary tears apart the Iron Curtain and turns to democratic government and a free economy. The country becomes part of the EU in 2004.

Sightseeing

As with any great city, Budapest has far too many attractions to cover in a short time. If you can, it is ideal to wander round at leisure and get to know the city by degrees. The best place to start is in Buda.

The Castle District

This fascinating zone of cobbled streets, hidden gardens and medieval courtyards hovers over the rest of Budapest on a long, narrow plateau. Towering gracefully above the old town is the neo-Gothic spire of the **Matthias Church**. Founded in the 13th century by King Béla IV, it has witnessed many dramatic events: the excommunication of a Pope, the splendid wedding of Matthias Corvinus to Beatrice of Aragon and the coronation in 1867 of the Austrian Emperor Franz Joseph as King of Hungary. The building itself is essentially 19th-century neo-Gothic, attached to what the Turks left of the original edifice in 1686. The **Loreto Chapel** contains the revered statue of the Virgin once buried by the Turks in the chapel walls. It is said to have reappeared miraculously during the siege of 1686.

Nearby rises an undulating white rampart with gargoyles and cloisters: the **Fishermen's Bastion**. Built on the site of a medieval fish market, it recalls the fact that in the 18th century local fishermen were responsible for defending the fortifications. The present Disneyesque structure dates from early in the 20th century. The arches frame the river artistically, as if they had been designed especially for photographers.

Looking west, you face the tinted glass façade of the **Hilton Hotel**. The building incorporates the remains of a 17th-century Jesuit college and a 13th-century abbey. In the lobby is an ancient milestone, found on the site, which once marked the limit of the Roman Empire.

The Castle District is only four streets wide and easily covered on foot. As you walk around, it is worth peeking into the big doorways to discover otherwise hidden architectural details, such as sculpted stone seats. In 1800 Beethoven stayed in the baroque mansion at No. 7 Táncsics Mihály utca. This was the Jewish quarter until the 16th century; the house now contains the Museum of Music History.

The main road, Országház utca, was once called the street of baths. Many medieval features remain. At No. 2, a restaurant occupies a grand 15th-century mansion with a cloistered courtyard. The street leads into

Tárnok utca, which contains some fine baroque buildings. Úri utca is also a treasure trove of picturesque medieval vestiges. Along the western ramparts runs the Tóth Árpád sétány promenade, offering panoramas over the Buda Hills.

Generations of spires punctuate the sky over the Castle District.

The Royal Palace

After a long and turbulent history, including complete destruction after World War II, the palace begun in the 13th century by Béla IV was restored to its former splendour and offers a delightful view over Pest and the Danube from its walls. The building houses three excellent museums. In the baroque south wing, the **History Museum** evokes the city's evolution since the Bronze Age. Downstairs in the excavated part of the medieval castle you can see a roomful of striking Gothic statues unearthed in 1974. The **Hungarian National Gallery**, an impressive modern exhibition of Hungarian art from the Middle Ages to the present day, occupies the centre under the dome. You enter from the terrace overlooking the Danube.

The **Museum of Contemporary Art** (Ludwig Collection) puts on temporary exhibitions, while its huge collection is rotated regularly, so you can never be sure whether you will see works by Picasso, Baselit, Lichtenstein, Warhol or Hungarian artists such as Endre Tót, Molnár and Erdély.

Danube Views

Gellért Hill, right alongside the Danube, takes its name from an Italian missionary (Gerard) who converted the Hungarians but was eventually thrown from the hill in a barrel spiked with nails, in 1046, by militant heathens. The summit is dominated by the severe-looking **Citadel**. Built in the mid-19th century, it served in World War II as the last stronghold of the German occupying army. A conspicuous modern addition to the hilltop is the **Liberation Monument**, visible from many parts of the city. While most Soviet-inspired statuary was transferred to Szoborpark, on the city outskirts, after the collapse of communism, the gigantic woman brandishing a palm frond was considered too important a part of the skyline to jettison.

Down below, riverside Buda is known as Watertown because of its thermal baths. **Rudas Baths**, one of the most colourful, has been in business since 1556.

At the Buda side of the Chain Bridge (Szechenyi Lánchid), a **funicular** reaches Castle Hill just north of the Royal Palace gates. It provides one of the most scenic rides in Budapest, and has been in operation since 1870. A short walk north of the Chain Bridge, in Batthyány tér, the twin-towered **St Anne's Church** is one of the most striking baroque structures in the city. Designed by a Jesuit,

Ignatius Pretelli, in Italian style in the mid-18th century, the interior is a dazzling drama of huge statues and black marble columns.

Continuing from the square up Fő utca, you reach another 16th-century Turkish bath, the **Király Gyógyfürdő**, with a stone dome and octagonal pool. Further along is the **Gül Baba Türbéje**, still another relic of the Turkish era. The meticulously preserved tomb was built over the grave of a renowned dervish.

Óbuda

North of Buda, surrounded by concrete highrises, busy roads and flyovers, are the remains of **Aquincum**, which developed from legionnaires' camp to the Roman capital of Lower Pannonia.

There's an amphitheatre on the corner of Nagyszombat utca and Pacsirtamező út, and military baths near the Árpád híd train station, but they have not been well maintained. The calmest spot in which to dwell on the Roman past is at the **Aquincum Museum**, built on the site of the main civil town. It displays excavated items and a model of what the town would have looked like.

Afterwards, explore the cobbled squares of central Óbuda, enlivened by cafés, restaurants and galleries. In a fine old mansion on Szentlélek tér, next to the Árpad Híd station, the **Vasarely Museum** displays more than 350 works of the Op Art pioneer.

Margaret Island

When the Romans were exhausted by the wear and tear of life in Aquincum, *Margit sziget* is where they came to rest. Comprising mostly parkland, woods and gardens, Margaret Island is an almost traffic-free haven of beauty and peace in the middle of the Danube. Probably like the Romans, today's visitors put the accent on culture both physical and cerebral, enjoying a sporting complex, thermal baths and an open-air theatre. Near the theatre, wander through the ruins of the 13th-century **Dominican convent** founded by Béla IV, where his daughter Margaret spent most of her life.

Pest

Across the river there are no hills to climb, but the busy streets and imposing boulevards offer plenty to see. The oldest surviving structure in Pest, nestled against the flyover leading to Elizabeth Bridge, is the **Inner City Parish Church**. Founded in the 12th century, it served

CENTRAL BUDAPEST

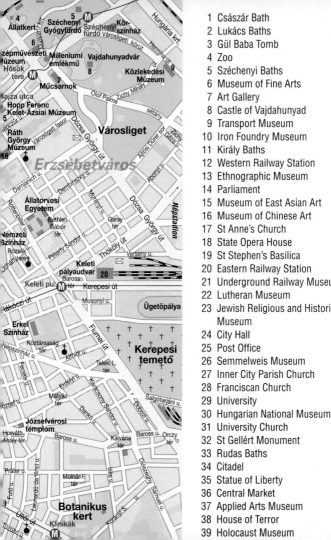

some time as a mosque under the Turkish occupation, and a Muslim prayer niche is still to be seen near the altar. In the adjacent square, Március 15. tér, a sunken park displays the excavations of the Roman outpost **Contra-Aquincum**.

The cobbled centrepiece of an expansive pedestrian zone, **Váci utca** is packed with shops selling local wine and food, art and antiques, cosmetics, fashion and jewellery. Street vendors hawk all manner of goods. There are several cafés and restaurants where you can sit back and contemplate the street's eclectic architectural mix, up above the shopfronts.

Towards the Chain Bridge at **Martinelli tér**, stand back and admire the square's Art Nouveau architecture.

Vestiges of the city's medieval walls have been attractively incorporated into more recent buildings, notably in the streets that form part of the **Kiskörút** boulevard, bending its way from the Szabadság Bridge to Deák tér, and changing names along the way. One of its most fascinating landmarks is at 1 Vámház körút, a cavernous red-brick and cast-iron **covered market**, full of local colour and exotic smells. It opened in 1897. The ground floor is crammed with food stalls selling every conceivable ingredient for a gourmet Hungarian meal, while upstairs are as many souvenir and novelty stalls as you could ever want in one place.

The Múzeum körút section is dominated by the **Hungarian National Museum**, with a magnificent neoclassical façade. The huge exhibition is imaginatively designed and covers the entire drama of the nation's history, from the settlement of the Magyars in the Carpathian Basin to the collapse of communism and advent of democracy more than a thousand years later. The highlight is the beautiful Hungarian crown jewels, displayed separately in their own darkened room. The cross on the top of the crown was bent when the jewels were smuggled out of the country to escape the Mongols. They eventually found their way to Fort Knox and were restored to Hungary only in 1978.

Vámház körút and Múzeum körút intersect at Kálvin tér, where you might wish to make a foray into Üllői út to visit the building truly pulsating with shocks that houses the **Museum of Applied Arts**. The style of the brick-and-ceramic-tile palace is listed as Art Nouveau, though it might be better described as Fantasy Hungarian with strong eastern influences.

The exhibits tell a terse history of ceramics in China, Europe and, in particular, Hungary. Also on show are furniture, textiles, oriental rugs, metalwork, clocks and curios made by extremely talented Hungarian and foreign hands.

Further south, on Páva útca, the **Holocaust Museum** was inaugurated in 2004. This memorial includes a long-abandoned synagogue that has been magnificently renovated, as well as a new complex with exhibition halls, conference rooms, offices and research centre. Permanent and temporary exhibitions relate events leading up to the Hungarian holocaust through photos, films and documents.

On Dohány utca you will see the twin onion-domed towers of the Central Synagogue, the biggest in Europe and built in a strange oriental-Byzantine style. Within the complex is the **Jewish Museum**, reflecting many centuries of Jewish life in Hungary. It houses some spine-chilling documents on the fate of the Budapest ghetto in World War II.

At the Deák tér end of the boulevard, the **Metro Museum,** in the station, recounts the building of the Millennial Railway.

Continuing on from Deák tér is Bajcsy-Zsilinszky út, one of the boulevards that give the city

its Parisian air. On the west side towers the city's largest church, **St Stephen's Basilica**. Under construction from 1851–1905, it was worked on by three successive architects, in as many different styles. Its most revered relic is the mummified right hand of St Stephen, kept in a silver reliquary.

To the northwest along the embankment, the **Houses of Parliament** symbolize the grandeur of the Austro-Hungarian Empire, looking much like their British counterpart.

HUNGARIAN FOLK ART

Hungary's rich folk art tradition means there are plenty of colourful souvenirs of the country to take home. Hungarian wood-carving is always popular—especially striking are Hussar chess sets painted in the bright colours of the famous brigade's uniforms. Equally brilliant are top-quality hand-worked textiles, such as embroidered blouses, jackets, carpets and bed linen. The best places to look for these items are the stalls on the first floor of the **Great Market Hall** and the boutique called **Judit** on Tárnok utca. Good speciality stores dealing in textiles include **Anna Antikvitás** along Falk Miksa utca, Budapest's main street for antique shops.

Be sure to take a stroll along the most stately avenue in Budapest, **Andrássy út**, modelled after the Champs-Elysées in the 1870s. Its name has been changed many times, but by any title this remains a spacious, patrician thoroughfare. Stop in at the **Postal Museum** at No. 3, which has a surprisingly entertaining collection of curiosities.

The neo-Renaissance **State Opera House** is the most admired building on the avenue. Statues of 16 great composers stand high above the entrance, with Franz Liszt and Ferenc Erkel in places of honour.

The **House of Terror** is located at no. 60. In 1944, this building (called the House of Loyalty at the time) was the seat of the Hungarian national-socialist party. From 1945 to 1956, the Communist secret police used it for interrogations, torture and executions. In 2001–02 the building was transformed into a memorial illustrating the methods of the two 20th century reigns of terror, through photographs and audio documents. At no. 103, the **Ferenc Hopp Museum of Asiatic Art** displays splendid collections of Chinese Buddhist sculptures, Indian paintings, Japanese silks and so on, amassed by a wealthy businessman.

The avenue ends with a flourish at the vast and airy **Heroes' Square**, with the Millenary

PORCELAIN

High-quality Hungarian arts and crafts have a long history, especially in ceramics and porcelain. Items made from these materials have become the most sought-after products for visitors to Hungary. Two names in particular stand out. The Herend Porcelain Factory is based in the town of Herend near Lake Balaton and has been making exquisite hand-painted vases, dishes, bowls and statuettes since 1826. Herend has proved especially popular with royalty—satisfied customers include Queen Victoria, Kaiser Wilhelm I, the Shah of Iran and Prince Charles. Find out why at the main Herend shop just behind Vörösmarty tér on V. József Nádor tér 11.

Zsolnay porcelain might not be able to boast as famous a client list, but its products have been far more prominently placed. The company developed a line in brilliant weatherproof ceramic tiles in the late 19th century, and these adorn the rooftops of Matthias Church, the Central Market and the Museum of Applied Arts. Check out their modern Art Nouveau-influenced designs at V. Kígyó utca 4.

Monument as its centrepiece, topped by statue of the Archangel Gabriel. Begun on the thousandth anniversary of the Magyar conquest, the monument depicts Prince Árpád and his chieftains enclosed in a colonnade of Hungary's most illustrious leaders, ranging from King Stephen I to Kossuth, the 1848 revolutionary.

Facing each other across the expanse of Heroes' Square are two almost identical neoclassical buildings. The larger one is the **Museum of Fine Arts**, whose comprehensive collection of paintings, including a number of French Impressionists, makes it an institution of international importance. The smaller clone, the **Art Gallery**, houses temporary exhibitions of paintings by Hungarian and foreign artists.

Beyond the Millenary Monument sprawls the vast **City Park**. Among its amenities is an artificial lake and the extraordinary Castle of Vajdahunyad, modelled on a Transylvanian castle. In front of the main doorway sits the hooded statue of a royal scribe known only as Anonymous, who wrote the first Hungarian chronicles. The figure of George Washington was presented to Budapest in 1906 by Hungarian settlers in the United States.

East of the castle, **Petőfi Hall** has an arena for rock concerts and discos, a Museum of Aviation and Space Travel, and a weekend flea market.

Across from the park rises the triple dome of the **Széchenyi Baths**, one of Europe's largest medicinal bath complexes. The amusing sight of people industriously playing chess while soaking in the healing waters is not to be missed.

Excursions

Some 30 km (18 miles) south of Budapest, the town of **Gödöllö** is particularly known for its castle. In 1867, when the emperor Franz Joseph I of Austria and his wife Elisabeth (Sissi) were crowned King and Queen of Hungary, they received the castle as a wedding gift.

The royal pair's regular visits gave the region a new significance. The empress came often, delighted to escape from the stiff etiquette of Vienna and to practise her favourite sport, horse riding. The castle, built from 1744 to 1748 by Andreas Mayerhoffer, was renovated in 1997. Tours include the state rooms, the park and the stables.

Also known as the Great Plain (Nagyalföld), the vast, flat prairie of the **Puszta** was Hungary's very own Wild West during the 19th century, when huge herds of cattle grazed here watched over by cowboys, called *gulyás*. It was once covered in thick forest, but was laid waste during the Turkish occupation, because of the invaders' need for timber to build fortresses, and became a virtual desert. Its renaissance as pastureland was due to the irrigation works on the River Tisza employed by Count Széchenyi in the early 19th century. But by the 20th century, the success of the irrigation scheme meant it could sustain crop development, and big landowners carried out wholesale enclosure, killing off the cattle industry and creating widespread poverty among the peasants. Under post-war communism, the estates were nationalized, and huge collective farms introduced, only to be broken up after 1989 and returned to private ownership.

Today, you will find pleasant little towns—Kecskemét and Szeged in particular are worth spending time in—beyond which are attractive old whitewashed farmsteads adorned with bright-coloured strings of paprika.

Balaton is one of the largest lakes in Europe. It is strikingly elongated, stretching for 77 km (48 miles) along the foothills of the Bakony Mountains, but only 14 km (8.7 miles) across at its widest point. It is also remarkably shallow—a mere 11 m (36 ft) at its maximum depth. This has some interesting side effects. It freezes over completely in winter, making it one of the world's great skating rinks, while in summer the water heats up like a thermal bath. The bottom is soft and sandy; your feet stir up brown clouds of silt. The lake's shallowness also makes it vulnerable to strong winds, which can create high waves in a matter of minutes.

The lakewater is packed with minerals which, given the Hungarian love of spas, means there are a number of health resorts. Balatonfüred, on the northeast shore, has been frequented for its medicinal springs for the last 250 years.

Dining Out

A popular appetizer is *libamáj-pástétom*, flaky pastry filled with goose-liver pâté. *Hortobágyi húsos palacsinta* are pancakes filled with minced meat and sour cream; *gombafejek rántva*, breadcrumb-coated fried mushrooms. Now for the goulash, which is not at all a spicy stew, but a thinnish soup. Called *gulyásleves*, it combines bits of beef, vegetables, caraway seeds and paprika for colour and zing.

Szegedi halászlé is a freshwater fish soup. On a hot day, cold fruit soups *(hidegyümölcsleves)*, made from cherries or apricots, are very refreshing.

For the fish course, try *paprikás ponty*, carp with a paprika sauce; *rácponty*, carp stew with sour cream; or *pisztráng tejszín mártásbán*, baked trout with cream.

Hungarians are extremely fond of large helpings of meat. *Pörkölt* or *bográcsgulyás* is the spicy stew that non-Hungarians call "goulash". On menus you'll see *paprikás csirke*, chicken with sour cream and paprika. *Töltött paprika* are stuffed peppers; *bélszin Budapest módra* is a thick beef steak served with a sauce of peppers, mushrooms, peas and chopped chicken livers.

The Hungarians excel in the dessert department, so be sure to save room for a strudel *(rétes)* filled with *almás* (apple), *mákos* (poppy seeds), *meggyes* (sour cherries) or *túrós* (lemon, raisins and cottage cheese); or *Gundel palacsinta*, pancakes with a rich filling of chopped walnuts and raisins, cov-

ered in chocolate sauce and flambéed with brandy or rum. For more simple tastes, there is always ice cream *(fagylalt)* or fruit *(gyümölcs)*.

Shopping

For starters, you will surely want to return home with some of the world-famous hand-painted Herend porcelain, ranging from a tiny flower-patterned brooch or an adorable little snail with gilded shell to a full dinner service. Here are some other good buys.

Articles crafted from copper, brass or silver; rustic hand-carved wood articles and leather goods. Handmade carpets and rugs in traditional patterns; embroidered shirts and blouses; finely embroidered linenware. Cotton or paper sachets of ground paprika; spicy dried sausage; a garland of dried cherry peppers; packaged cake or strudel; a bottle of wine or fruit brandy. Finally, CDs and tapes: Liszt, Kodály and Bartók in a variety of recordings; gypsy violins and folk music.

Climate. The city can become very hot and humid, especially in July and August when many town dwellers head for the cooler shores of Lake Balaton. Winters are cold. The best weather is in May and September, when Budapest is pleasantly mild and fairly crowd-free.

Currency. The *forint* (Ft.) is issued in coins from 1 to 100 Ft. and banknotes from 200 to 20,000 Ft. Retain all currency exchange receipts to re-exchange forints when leaving the country. Do not change money on the street. Many tourist-oriented establishments accept international credit cards, and US dollars are accepted even on market stalls.

Driving. Budapest is difficult to navigate as there are no left turns, and the roads are not in perfect condition, with on-going repairs everywhere. Better take a taxi, and try to agree on a fare before you set off.

Opening hours. *Banks* are generally open Monday to Friday 9 a.m.–2 p.m., until noon on Saturdays. *Post offices*, Monday to Friday 8 a.m.–6 p.m. Saturdays to 2 p.m.; the main post office and those in the east and west railway stations are open round the clock. *Shops* are usually open 10 a.m.–6 p.m. (Thursdays to 8 p.m.); food shops as early as 6 or 7 a.m.

Safety. Although crime levels have risen since the fall of communism, Budapest remains a fairly safe city by Western standards. It is nonetheless worth taking some basic precautions. Only carry the money you will need for the day along with a credit card. Watch out for pickpockets in tourist areas and on public transport, and beware of scams aimed at foreigners along Váci utca, which will end up with you and your money parting company.

Sales tax. A tax of 16 per cent is imposed on goods in Hungary. To benefit from a tax refund, your purchase in any one store must amount to a minimum of 50,000 Ft. Ask the sales assistant for a fiscal invoice, a VAT Reclaim form and a tax-free envelope. Keep all receipts for currency exchange and your credit card slips, and when you leave the country, have all these documents stamped by a Hungarian Customs Officer. Shops offering this service display a Tax-Free Shopping logo.

Tipping. Waiters and taxi drivers expect a tip of 10–15 per cent.

Transport. The Budapest Transport Company (BKV) runs a large network of buses, trams and trolleybuses as well as three metro lines and, in summer, a ferry service on the Danube. The system is efficient, reliable, good value and gets you within walking distance of just about all the main sights. Most public transport starts at around 4.30 a.m. and goes on till 11.30 p.m. Maps of the system can be bought at the main metro and railway stations.

BELGRADE

Gateway to the Levant

Belgrade (Beograd), capital of Serbia, is one of four capital cities on the banks of the Danube. Along with Vienna, Bratislava and Budapest, it was a crucial site in Europe's commercial and communications network even before Roman times. In fact it was settled as far back as the Bronze and Early Iron ages, and the Celts built a fortress there in the 3rd century BC.

When the Roman Empire was split into East and West in 395, the seat of power moved from Rome to Constantinople. Byzantium was allotted Belgrade in its portion, and the boundary between the two parts of the empire ran beneath the city walls. The division is still mirrored in Belgrade's adherence to the Orthodox faith, which evolved throughout Byzantium. The Byzantines were not alone in coveting Belgrade. Bulgars, Hungarians, Austrians and Turks all held it over the ages. The Turks left only in 1867, and if you keep your eyes open, you will sense the Orient's sway.

Not surprisingly, the city has turned its back on the Danube, which brought it so much grief. It faces a tributary, the more modest Sava. The city was badly bombed in the two world wars of the 20th century, and because of its strategic situation was occupied by Austria and Germany. Apart from the ancient fortress that has known so many masters, little of Belgrade is really old.

The postwar period has seen the change from a small Balkan town to a modern European metropolis, with a population of more than 1.6 million, capital of the newly formed State of Serbia and Montenegro (and now just Serbia). In rebuilding, the emphasis was placed on the scientific, educational, cultural and conference infrastructure. The people are proud of their reputation in these spheres; they are, understandably, less happy about the political arena and the problems its leaders have made for them in recent years by stirring up war in Bosnia. But with some of the international economic sanctions now lifted and despite the assassination of Prime Minister Zoran Djindic in 2003, Belgrade is looking forward to a brighter future. The new president Boris Tadic, leader of the Democratic Party, promised to commit Serbia to membership of the EU. In March 2006, the former President Milošević, arrested for war crimes, died in The Hague before the end of his trial.

A BRIEF HISTORY

1st–7th centuries AD	The Romans capture and rebuild the Celtic settlement (which they name Singidunum) during the 1st century AD. When the Roman empire is divided in two in 395, Belgrade is situated in the Eastern part under the authority of Constantinople. From the 5th to 7th centuries the town is sacked by barbarian tribes, including the Goths, the Avars and the Huns. The Slavs move into the region towards the end of this period and rebuild on the ruins. They give it the name Beli Grad, "White City".
8th–15th centuries	The town is fought over for centuries by Franks, Byzantines, Bulgars and Hungarians. In 1284 it comes into the hands of the Serbian king Draguti and is made capital of the kingdom of Serbia in 1402 under the despot Stefan Lazarević.
16th–19th centuries	In 1521 Belgrade falls to the Turks, who remain for three centuries (although the Austrians capture it several times for brief periods). It is the Turks' chief western bastion after they are driven back from Vienna and Budapest; they are definitively forced out in 1867.
20th century– present day	After World War I, the South Slav peoples unite to form the kingdom of the Serbs, Croats and Slovenes (later the kingdom of Yugoslavia); Belgrade is its capital. Early in World War II, the city is again heavily bombed by the Germans, and later they seize it. After the war the communist Josip Broz Tito rules over a newly constituted socialist republic. In 1990 Slobodan Milošević rises to the presidency. In 1992 the federation disintegrates, leaving Serbia and Montenegro alone in a shrunken Yugoslavia.For Milošević's efforts in inspiring the war in Bosnia, the UN imposes economic sanctions. At the end of 1996 Milošević annuls election results favouring the opposition, provoking civic unrest. In 1997 he becomes President of the Federal Republic of Yugoslavia; the following year the situation in the Kosovo worsens and Serbia begins offensive against the separatists in May; NATO retaliates by bombing Belgrade. In 1999 a peace deal is brokered. In 2000 Milošević is forced to resign. The State of Serbia and Montenegro is established in 2003, and Montenegro votes for independence in 2006.

Sightseeing

Looming over the meeting point of the Danube and the Sava is the old **fortress** with its upper and lower towns. On the hill, offering wide views over the two rivers, the Romans built their fortifications in the 1st century AD, as did a Byzantine emperor several centuries later. When the Austrians occupied the fortress in 1717–39, after temporarily dislodging the Turks, they made it one of the mightiest bastions of all Europe. Today the citadel and its military museum, the Roman well, Turkish hamams, churches, ancient ramparts, towers and gates all speak reams of the passage of time and the multitude of invaders. As a strange twist of fate, the large plateau surrounding the fortress has been turned into a pleasant park, **Kalemegdan**, with a zoo, children's amusement park, sports grounds and restaurants.

Further along the Sava, just outside the fortress, is the old quarter of *Varoš kapija* (City Gate), where you'll find the 19th-century **Belgrade Cathedral** (*Saborna crkva*), erected across from the Patriarch's residence, the Museum of the Serbian Orthodox Church and the House of Princess Ljubica. The cathedral used to house the ven-

erated relics of Prince Lazar. He came to a sorry end in 1389, during Serbia's golden age of expansion. In a battle against the Turks on the plain of Kosovo, he lost most of his army—as well as his head, lopped off by a scimitar. Other emperors and rulers are buried under the altar or in the crypt, making the cathedral a monument to the great men of Serbian history.

The **House of Princess Ljubica**, a pretty white mansion, was built for her in 1831 by her husband, Prince Miloš Obrenović. Full of antique furniture and ornaments, its Turkish baths, oriental carpets and floor-level seating show how the Turks influenced the lifestyle of the Serbian rulers.

Running southeast of the fortress, the old Roman road to the south, **Knez Mihailova Street**, is now a pedestrian area. You can stroll past shops and art galleries right through to Terazije Square. At the end of the street is Republic Square, where you'll find the **National Museum**. This institution displays everything from prehistoric weapons, jewellery retrieved from archaeological digs, icons and religious books, as well as Serbian and European art. As most of the city's monuments were devastated during the two world wars, only the

museums safeguard its historical memories. Visit the **Ethnographic Museum**, devoted to Serbian arts and folklore, and the **Fresco Gallery**, which reproduces stunning religious murals found in monasteries all over ex-Yugoslavia.

The **Museum of Modern Art** is situated across the Sava River in Novi Beograd, in an otherwise uninteresting area. However, north of Novi Beograd, the quiet quarter of **Zemun** is worth a visit: stately 18th- and 19th-century residences echo the prosperity forged here by the Austrians, at the far limit of their territories during the three centuries the Turks kept them out of Belgrade.

Looking back over the city, towards the Vračar plateau, you can't miss the dome of **St Sava Cathedral** which dominates the skyline. Construction began in the early 20th century, to be completed only in 1995. This is the largest Orthodox church in the world, big enough to hold a congregation of 12,000. Belgrade is, in fact, a city of many places of worship, most of them Eastern Orthodox churches, but there is also a synagogue, the Bajrakli Mosque and several Roman Catholic churches.

After you have explored the city, you may well have the feeling that everything is still haunted by the tragic Serbian past. Switch to a lighter mood

by spending a few hours in the old bohemian district known as **Skadarlija**. Here among the numerous small art galleries you'll meet painters selling their canvasses, roving actors, fortune-tellers and musicians, all in a good-humoured atmosphere. The traditional music played in the cosy restaurants and wine houses goes on until the small hours.

Excursions

Popular excursions from Belgrade include a visit to nearby **Topčider** with its lovely park and the historic palace of Prince Miloš Obrenović, and to **Mount Avala** with its Monument to the Unknown Soldier at the top.

History buffs will no doubt enjoy a trip to **Topola**. A small fort marks the spot where Karadjordje, or Black George, the leader of the 1804–13 insurrection against the Turks, had his home. He is buried here in the richly decorated St George's church. Close by is **Arandjelovac**, a spa town at the edge of the forest, boasting a pleasant park and open-air sculpture museum.

Dining Out

Belgrade's cuisine reflects the influence of many cultures: Turkish and Austro-Hungarian dishes feature on the menu alongside traditional Serbian favourites.

Weather permitting, a leisurely meal on one of the many raft or river-boat restaurants is a delightfully relaxing way to spend an evening. For music in an arty atmosphere, head for the Skadarlija quarter.

Pršut (raw ham) or *salama*, a kind of salami, make good starters, as does *pasulj* (Serbian bean soup with smoked pork and peppers) or *gulaš* soup, a spicy broth with chunks of beef of Hungarian origin.

Main dishes are *ćevapčići* (grilled spicy fingers of minced meat), *pljeskavice* (meat patties), *ražnjići* (skewers of grilled meat, optionally served with sauerkraut), *sarma* (stuffed cabbage, vine leaves or peppers), *musaka* (which you'll know if you've been to Greece as moussaka: oven-baked layers of minced meat and slices of potato, aubergine or courgettes). *Srpska salata* (Serbian salad), sliced tomatoes and onion, usually comes with the main dish; out of season it may be pickles of various kinds. If you long for fresh perch from the Danube, then head for the Zemun quarter, known for its good fish restaurants.

If you have a sweet tooth, end your meal with a wedge of 121 *baklava*, a flaky pastry filled with walnuts and oozing honey. *Palačinke* are pancakes with various fillings such as jam, chopped walnuts and chocolate sauce, or ice-cream. Poppy-seed *strudel* is another good dessert, though not exactly light.

Drinks

Sremski Karlovci, near Novi Sad, is reputed for its excellent wines. To simplify communication with the waiter, learn the words *bjelo* for white, *crno* for red.

The most famous spirits are *šljivovica* and *lozovača*, distilled from plums and grapes respectively.

Shopping

An excellent idea for a Serbian souvenir is an oriental-style carpet, a legacy from the long Turkish occupation. Transport should not be a problem, providing you choose something reasonably small. Carpets are either hand-loomed or machine-made, with prices to correspond.

Wood carvings (in the form of statuettes, chess sets or salad sets), embroidery and lace are good value for money. Leather articles—handbags, wallets, belts, jackets—are plentiful, but it's best to look around before you make that final purchase.

PRACTICAL INFORMATION

Credit cards and travellers cheques. In general, travellers cheques can be cashed in large banks, hotels or issuing agencies. Credit cards are accepted in few places.

Currency. The Serbian dinar (CSD) is divided into 100 paras. Coins from 50 paras to 20 dinars, notes from 10 to 5000 dinars. The Euro is accepted (it is legal tender in Montenegro).

Dress code. When visiting churches and monasteries, no shorts or mini-skirts are allowed. Women are expected to cover their heads, while men should remove their hats.

Opening hours. *Banks*: 7 a.m. to 3 p.m., Monday to Friday. Some branches also open Saturday from 8 a.m. to 2 p.m. *Shops*: 8 a.m. to noon and 5 p.m. to 8 p.m., Monday to Friday, and 8 a.m. to 3 p.m. on Saturday. The larger shops in cities and tourist areas do not close at midday.

Tipping. In hotels, restaurants and taxis, a 10% tip is customary.

Tourist Information. Pedestrian underpass in Terazije Square.

Water. Tap water is chlorinated and safe for drinking, but bottled mineral water tates better.

BUCHAREST

Visions of Grandeur

In the southeast of Romania, less than 50 km (30 miles) from Bulgaria, Bucharest is the political, economical and cultural centre of the country, in the heart of Walachia. The town spreads along the banks of the Dâmbovița, a tributary of the Danube, and the first written documents mentioning the city were signed by Prince Vlad Țepeș "the Impaler", ruler of Walachia and model for Dracula, on September 20, 1459.

Over the centuries the city endured several dark periods, beginning with its destruction by the Turks in 1595. In 1659, it became capital of Walachia then, two centuries later (1862), of the principality formed by the reunion of Walachia and Moldavia. It was designated capital of the Kingdom of Romania in 1881.

During its golden age, between the two world wars, the city was redesigned by French and Romanian architects trained in Paris. The streets were transformed into tree-lined boulevards, a triumphal arch was erected, earning Bucharest the title of "Little Paris of the East". Despite bombing in 1944 and the Communist policy of urbanizationwhich totally ignored aesthetics, then an earthquake in 1977, not to mention the destruction of the charming old districts by Nikolae Ceausescu, Bucharest has retained its own special atmosphere. Its leafy parks, lively café terraces and charming old churches bring glimmers of light into the urban greyness. The main sights can easily be reached on foot, by taxi or in the metro.

Of Romania's 22 million inhabitants, 2.1 million live in Bucharest, most of them in the wide belt of faceless apartment buildings encircling the city centre. The vast majority (87 per cent) are Orthodox, devoutly so despite—perhaps because of—45 years of Communist régime. (The Church was deprived of its wealth and the clergy put on a State salary.)

After the carefully orchestrated revolution that brought Romania to the international headlines in December 1989, the people are still trying to find their feet. They survived the hardships imposed by Ceausescu's personality cult, thanks to their self-deprecating sense of humour and an ability to always manage, somehow. You'll find them cheerful and friendly, and eager to talk to strangers. The name of their capital comes from Bucur: "happy". Don't criticize it too much; they love it, warts and all.

2nd–9th centuries AD	Legions of the Roman emperor Trajan are stationed in the territory of the Thracian tribe of the Dacians. The Romanian nation is formed through the union of the Romans and the native population of this territory, approximately equivalent to modern-day Romania.
13th–14th centuries	Hungarians establish their suzerainty over Walachia and Moldavia, organized as semi-autonomous provinces. A feudal system of prince, magnates (boyars), freemen and serfs develops. A walled city, Bucharest, is founded on the Walachian plains, on the site of a Roman fortress.
15th–17th centuries	Turkish suzerainty is accepted in the early 15th century. The Turks destroy the city in 1595 and a new, larger wall is built. In 1659 Bucharest becomes the capital of the principality of Walachia.
18th–19th centuries	The city changes hands frequently, being ruled in turn by Turks, Russians and Austrians. In 1862 it becomes capital of the newly created kingdom formed by the union of Walachia and Moldavia.
20th century–present	Upon the capitulation of the Central Powers in 1918, Bucharest becomes the capital of a much enlarged Romania. The new city, based on the Parisian model, is the target of Axis bombings on August 24, 1944, the day after Romania accepted Allied armistice terms. King Michael is forced to abdicate in 1947 and the Romanian People's Republic is proclaimed. Nicolae Ceausescu, general secretary of the Communist party, becomes head of state in 1967. The chemical and electro-technical industries are greatly developed. After a visit to China in 1971, Ceausescu changes tactics. Through his determination to repay the national debt, he wrings the economy dry. His policy of "systemization", attempting to wipe out the difference between town and country, his destruction of the more charming parts of old Bucharest to make space for his own sumptuous palace, bring about his downfall in December 1989. In May 1990 Ion Iliescu, the former Communist Central Committee Secretary, is elected president by an 85 per cent majority. The Democrat Traian Basescu is elected in December 2004. Romania hopes to join the EU in 2007.

125

Sightseeing

Despite an earthquake in 1977, despite Ceausescu's unusual conception of town planning, the city centre has still retained some of its turn-of-the-century charm. There are parks and open-air café terraces enough to bring respite to sightseeing feet.

A long boulevard, Calea Victoriei, meanders through the city from south to north, from the banks of the Dâmboviţa near the National History Museum, to Piaţa Victoriei. It then becomes Şoseaua Kiseleff, straight as a die, leading to a Triumphal Arch built in 1935 to honour the Romanian army of World War I. All the main sights are situated along or close to this boulevard and another parallel to it, Bulevardul Magheru. But don't try walking its whole length; take a taxi (the trams and underground are a bit hard to handle unless you speak Romanian or have a guide).

The centre of town in the 16th and 17th centuries is known as the **Lipscani district**; the name was derived from Leipzig, from where goods were imported. The district is bounded by the river to the south, Calea Victoriei to the west, Mihail Kogalniceanu and Republicii avenues to the north, and dwindles away in the east beyond Bratianu avenue. The area is becoming much livelier since the return to democracy—boutiques, art galleries, bars and banks are flourishing along the paved streets, on the ground floors of buildings that are slightly the worse for wear.

Start your sightseeing in Old Bucharest at **Piaţa Unirii**. The square is about two-thirds of the way along Bulevardul Unirii, the senselessly long fountain-studded avenue culminating in Ceaucescu's huge palace. Near Piaţa Unirii stand the remains of **Curtea Veche** (Old Courtyard), the palace of Vlad Ţepeş, resi-

In the open-air museum, Muzeul Satului, you can get a good idea of Romanian village life.

dence of the princes of Walachia and the only vestige of the medieval city. It was built in the 15th century and expanded by Constantin Brancovan (1688–1714). Destroyed by fire and earthquake, it was abandoned in the 18th century. Little remains of the grand vaulted halls and the luxuriant gardens.

The **church of Curtea Veche**, on Iuliu Manui street, was founded in the middle of the 16th century during the reign of Prince Mircea Ciobanu. The Walachian princes were sworn in here. Opposite, **Hanul lui Manuc** is an inn built round

a central courtyard by an Armenian merchant in 1808.

Bucharest is graced by numerous churches; perhaps the most attractive is located just north of Piaţa Unirii. On the street of the same name, **Stavropoleos Church** was built in 1724 when Bucharest was governed by a Phanariot from Constantinople. The oriental influence is evident in the arabesques and arcades; the frescoes, portraits of saints, are painted in the icon style, with gold leaf. Generally the churches are only open during services (which are frequent). Try the door, you might be in 127

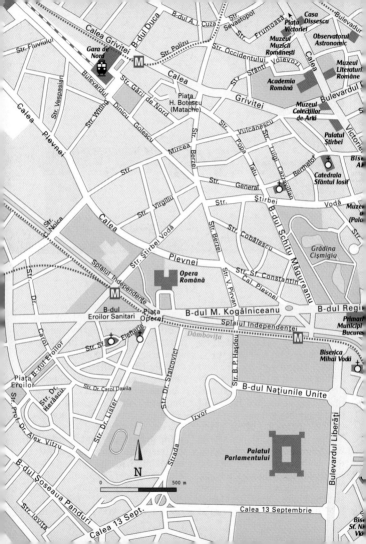

luck. In the same street, opposite the church, stands the old brasserie **Carul cu Bere** (literally, Beer Wagon), worth visiting just for its exuberant décor of painted woodwork, arched vaulting, frescoes and stained-glass windows. But it's also one of the best places in Bucharest for a good meal.

A short walk away, at the crossroads with Calea Victoriei, stands a pompous building that houses the **National History Museum**. It was originally the post office, built in neoclassical style in 1900. Among the many thousands of exhibits, the most interesting are the Daco-Roman collections, and the Treasury, presenting gold pieces from simple neolithic pieces to intricate Transylvanian jewellery of the 16th and 17th centuries.

Close by, **Pasajul Bijuteria**, a glass-roofed shopping arcade, stretches between Victoriei and Carada streets. It opens onto the National Bank, a fine neoclassical colonnaded affair taking up a whole block. The main entrance is on Lipscani street, the principal artery of the old district.

To the north, you can see the **National Library** in baroque style, and, on Ion Ghica Street, the Russian Orthodox church of **St Nicholas**, topped by several onion domes. Built from 1905 to 1909, it has a fine high altar and numerous icons. Near the entrance, note the tritons decorating the gutters.

Continue northwards to **Piaţa Universitatii**, one of the busiest squares of the city, dominated by the tower of the Intercontinental Hotel and the modern National Theatre (TNB).West of the square is the Second-Empire style university building and, in Enei street, the neo-Byzantine façade of the Ion Mincu Institute of Architecture.

On Bratianu Avenue, the little Şuţu Palace, a handsome neo-Gothic building enhanced by a wrought-iron and glass porch, was built from 1833 to 1835 for a Marshal of the court. It now houses the **Municipal Museum of Art and History**, tracing the development of the capital in photographs and other displays.

On the other side of the avenue, **Colţea church** dates from 1702. Its wooden door is carved with figures and winged horses.

Back on Piaţa Unirii, look along the esplanade covering the river, lined with boutiques and shopping centres. This was the former Avenue of the Victory of Socialism, 100 m wide, which the citizens referred to as Kitsch Boulevard during Ceaucescu's rule. At the far western end of the avenue is the enormous **Parliament Palace**, the house that Ceausescu built. Perched on top of an artificial hill riddled with secret passages and anti-atomic shelters, it is something of a national embarrassment. A fantasy of marble and gilt, it has 6000 rooms (second in size only to the Pentagon), secret passageways and nuclear shelters. To clear away the area for its construction, 40,000 inhabitants were displaced and a fifth of the old town was destroyed, including 19 churches, 9 of which were listed historic monuments. A team comprising 400 architects, 20,000 workers and soldiers was employed. Inside, the floors are marble, the walls lined with walnut and cherry panelling, the ceilings six storeys high, hung with monumental chandeliers. The infamous Ceaucescu couple never had time to enjoy their palace; it was still unfinished when they were executed in 1989. Since then the authorities have been trying to find a suitable role for the building; at present it is the seat of parliament, with a congress centre.

To get some idea of the appearance of the old Uranus district that Ceausescu bulldozed into oblivion, explore the streets directly south of Piaţa Unirii, around the **Patriarch's Church**, built in 1656, with three towers and a freestanding belltower. Closer to the Parliament Palace is the 18th-century **Antim Monastery**, its red-brick church covered with more recent mosaics.

In the west part of the city, the former bourgeois **Cotroceni district** has preserved several handsome houses, some of which have recently been restored. On the left bank of the river stands the Opera House, built in 1953 and surrounded by a pleasant park.

Further west, in a magnificent setting of wooded gardens, the **Cotroceni Palace** (access by Pr. Dr Gheorghe Marinescu Street) was built in 1893 by a French architect for Princess Marie, granddaughter of Queen Victoria and wife of King Ferdinand of Romania. It is partly open to the public and houses a museum known for its interesting medieval collections, as well as the residence of the President of the Republic.

Behind the palace, the **botanical garden** was created in 1884–85 and covers 17 ha planted with species from the world over. The garden is a favourite place for family outings at the weekend.

Calea Victoriei is one of the main thoroughfares, on a north-south axis. There are several museums and sites of interest on and around it. At the crossroads with Mihail Kogalniceanu Avenue stands the vast neoclassical building of the **Cercul Militar**; you can have a drink on the terrace.

A short walk westwards is the splendid **Grădina Cişmigiu**, considered Bucharest's most romantic park. It was created in 1860 around a lake, where you can hire a boat and enjoy the serenity of the weeping willows trailing their fronds in the water. To the south, through the branches, you can see the silhouette of the Town Hall.

Walking up Calea Victoriei you will see, on the left, the red-brick **Creţúlescu Church**, topped by two domes. Immediately behind it, on Revolution Square, is the imposing neoclassical building of the **National Art Gallery** on the corner of Strada Ştirbei Vodă. The building is the former Palace of the Republic, much damaged during the December Revolution, when the collections were severely depleted. Paintings by Romanian and European artists are displayed, in addition to works from the Far East.

Opposite stands the **Central University Library** with its neoclassical columns. On the same side of the street, the imposing **Ateneul Român**, beneath a great dome, was built between 1886 and 1888 by a French architect. The George Enescu Philharmonic Orchestra, named after the most famous Romanian composer and violinist, performs in the grand concert hall decorated by an immense fresco by the painter Costin Petrescu.

In the street between the Ateneul and the Library, the **Theodor Aman Museum** is located in the little pink house of the painter and engraver (1828–91), decorated with medallions and sculpted figures.

Further north, Calea Victoriei and the perpendicular streets are lined with numerous 19th-century buildings and several museums. At no. 111, the **Museum of Art Collections** displays paintings by Romanian artists and objets d'art from East and West.

Herăstrău Park, north of the Triumphal Arch, is not to be missed. Apart from shaded paths, several lakes and grassy lawns, the park contains the fascinating **Muzeul Satului**, founded in 1936 by Dimitrie Gusti, a professor of sociology. Called the Village and Folk Art Museum, it assembles 300 wooden buildings brought here from the four corners of Romania—farms, barns, thatched cottages, chalets, shepherd's huts, chapels, wells and windmills, all with their furnishings in the proper place, the bed linen, tablecloths, icons, down to the pots of basil on the windowsill. Push open a creaking door, and step into a forgotten world.

Dining Out

Romanian cuisine can be fairly described as hearty. Staples are potatoes and a corn mash similar to Italian polenta *(mamaliga)*, while the star of the meat department is pork. Many resourceful Romanians—even city dwellers—keep a pig for their sausage and bacon supplies. Food is bland rather than spicy, and vegetarians will not have an easy time.

Lunch often consists of soup: *bortsch*, made from beetroot and giblets; sour-tasting *ciorba*, based on fermented bran, with various additions such as tripe, potatoes, marrow-bones or chicken; *colesa*, made from boletus mushrooms.

At dinner, a large dish of cold meats, liver pâté and salami is often served as hors-d'œuvre.

The meat course may be tasty *sarmalés*, cabbage leaves stuffed with minced beef and rice, braised until golden and served with *mamaliga*; or roast chicken *(pui)* with fried potatoes and a sauce of crushed garlic, vinegar and water, or grilled cutlets *(muschiu)* of pork *(porc)* or beef *(vaca)*, with tiny pork sausages *(mititei)*.

Vegetables, served separately, are usually slices of aubergine or peppers braised in oil, or fat gherkins. Salads *(salata)* are rarely more varied than lettuce, tomato and cucumber.

Cheese is either yellow and compact *(cascaval)* or white and crumbly *(urda* or *brinza)*. Dessert may be fruit, ice cream, or, on special occasions, an elaborate gâteau with several layers of cream and frosted topping.

Drinks
Meals begin with a small glass of *tsuica*, a very heady plum brandy to be downed in one gulp to the cheer, *Noroc!*

Red and white wines are produced in the country. The best reds come from Murfatlar near Constanza—try the chardonnay. The best whites are the dry traminer or riesling or the sweet feteasca, all from Cotnari. With their meals Romanians tend to stick to the whites, often diluted with soda water.

The beer *(bere)* is a light lager. Bottled mineral water, *apa minerale*, is slightly fizzy. Soft drinks are sold straight from the crate at street stalls.

Coffee is served short, thick and strong, Turkish-style.

Shopping

Romanian girls are supposed to fill up their bottom drawer with their own crochet and embroidery work before they can hope to find a husband, and so traditional crafts have been maintained. Shops called Artizanat sell hand-embroidered table linen, but prices are high. The red woven scarves worn at Orthodox weddings make hard-wearing table runners or curtains.

Other interesting buys are brightly wood-carvings, icons and coloured ceramics.

PRACTICAL INFORMATION

Climate. Spring and autumn are moderate; winter is long (November to April) and cold, with a lot of snow. Summer is extremely hot and stuffy in Bucharest, cooler and more pleasant on the coast or in the mountains.

Courtesies. Romanian men have not lost the old-world habit of kissing a lady's hand when introduced. If you are invited into a Romanian's home, you should take a bouquet of flowers. Appreciated gifts are coffee beans and scented soap.

Currency. As of July 1, 2005, Romania dropped four zeros from its currency, the *leu* (plural *lei*). Both old *lei* (ROL) and new *lei* (RON) are in circulation until December 31, 2006. New notes: 1, 5, 10, 50, 100 and 500 *lei*. New coins: 1, 5, 10, and 50 *bani*. Only banks and authorized exchange offices can change foreign currency. There are automatic cash distributors in all the large towns. Keep all receipts as you may have to show them when leaving the country. International credit cards are accepted in good hotels, most restaurants and shops, and by hire car companies.

Language. Romanian, of Latin origin. Many words resemble Italian and French.

Opening Hours. Banks: Monday to Friday, 9 a.m.–noon and 1–3 p.m. Post offices: open Monday to Friday 8 a.m.–8 p.m., main ones also open Saturday to 2 p.m. Shops are generally open from 8 a.m. to 6 p.m. (Saturday to 1 p.m.), but department stores and some boutiques stay open until 8 p.m. or even later.

Taxis. By far the most convenient way of travelling around the city. State taxis are yellow and marked CAB. Make sure the meter is set at zero when you get in and switched on when you set off. Private taxis may not have a meter, so agree on the price beforehand. The drivers expect a tip.

Tipping. In restaurants the tip is often included; otherwise it is usual to leave around 10 per cent.

INDEX

INDEX

GENERAL EDITOR
Barbara Ender-Jones
PHOTO CREDITS
Hémisphères/Gardel: p. 1
Hémisphères/Wysocki: p. 103
Frédérique Fasser: pp. 2, 24, 30–31, 48, 71, 127
Dominique Michellod: p. 7
CORBIS.com: pp. 34, 50–51
CORBIS/Woolfitt: p. 55
CORBIS/Bianchetti: p. 59
Renata Holzbachová: pp. 75, 82, 89
© KunstHausWien: p. 87
R. Durous: p. 91
Marguerite Martinoli: pp. 97, 99, 113
Dragan Bosnic: p. 120
Claude Hervé-Bazin: p. 123
MAPS
Elsner & Schichor;
Huber Kartographie;
JPM Publications

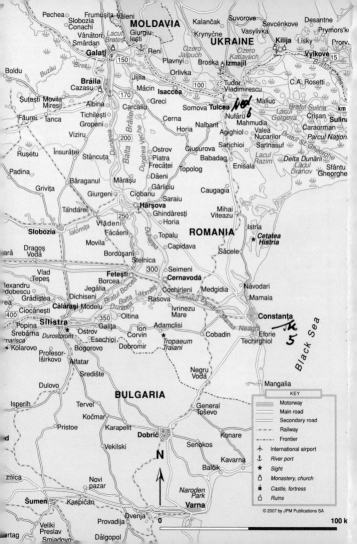